D1550341

Psychic Kids

True life stories of children
who see beyond the everyday

Sue Bishop

inspired
LIVING

ALLEN&UNWIN

First published in 2012

Copyright © Sue Bishop 2012

All rights reserved. No part of this book may be reproduced or transmitted in any
form or by any means, electronic or mechanical, including photocopying, recording
or by any information storage and retrieval system, without prior permission in
writing from the publisher. The Australian *Copyright Act 1968* (the Act) allows a
maximum of one chapter or 10 per cent of this book, whichever is the greater,
to be photocopied by any educational institution for its educational purposes
provided that the educational institution (or body that administers it) has given
a remuneration notice to Copyright Agency Limited (CAL) under the Act.

Inspired Living, an imprint of
Allen & Unwin
Sydney, Melbourne, Auckland, London

83 Alexander Street
Crows Nest NSW 2065
Australia
Phone: (61 2) 8425 0100
Fax: (61 2) 9906 2218
Email: info@allenandunwin.com
Web: www.allenandunwin.com

Cataloguing-in-Publication details are available from the
National Library of Australia www.trove.nla.gov.au

ISBN 978 1 74237 855 8

Internal design by Design by Committee
Set in 11.5/17.5 pt Electra LH by Post Pre-press Group, Australia
Printed and bound in Australia by the SOS Print + Media Group.

10 9 8 7 6 5 4

MIX
Paper from
responsible sources
FSC® C011217

The paper in this book is FSC® certified.
FSC® promotes environmentally responsible,
socially beneficial and economically viable
management of the world's forests.

Dedicated to Tristan and Chiara,
my awesome psychic kids

Contents

ACKNOWLEDGEMENTS

I'd like to thank my kids, Tristan and Chiara, for selecting me to be their mother in this lifetime. Their soul journey has taught me so much about the new generation of psychic kids.

I must admit that I really enjoyed writing this book because it gave me the opportunity to meet some truly amazing people who opened their souls to me. Thanks for spreading the love to help others embrace their psychic abilities.

I would like to give special thanks to Diana O'Shea for her wonderful feedback and assistance. I would also like to thank the fantastic team at Allen & Unwin—my publisher Maggie Hamilton, my publicist Anna Hayward, the editor Susin Chow, and Aziza Kuypers and Kathy Mossop.

Finally I'd like to thank my family, friends and students—you know how special you all are to me.

1
IS MY CHILD PSYCHIC?

There's a global phenomenon going on. You may have sensed it, others have too. Our kids are becoming more psychic. Why? It's because they're being born with an awareness that belies their age. These children stand out because many of them have the wisdom of old souls. It is this uniqueness that keeps us on our toes, because these kids don't come with a user manual. They are breaking all the rules of how things are meant to be. The psychic child is capable of crossing the boundaries between two worlds— our everyday world and the spirit world. And I can empathise with parents who feel they are not keeping pace with these changes.

Discovering that your child has amazing psychic abilities can be incredibly exciting. It can also be confronting when they see and hear things that you can't. As a parent, I know how concerned you might feel having to deal with it. As a psychic, I can appreciate what your child is going through.

Caitlin had an unsettling experience when her three-year-old Steven came running into the house.

'She won't play with me!' he cried.

'Who won't?' asked Caitlin.

'The little girl,' he replied.

Caitlin couldn't see anyone. 'What little girl?'

'That one out there,' he said, pointing to the courtyard.

They went outside together.

'Talk to her,' he demanded. 'Tell her to play with me.'

'Where is she?' Caitlin asked.

'Right there,' he cried, pointing in frustration. 'Look, I'll show you.' Steven grabbed a ball and threw it towards the corner of the courtyard.

'See!' he sobbed. 'She won't try to catch it.'

Caitlin didn't know how to explain to him that the little girl wasn't real.

Then his seven-year-old brother Robbie came out. 'Where is she, Steven?' he asked. When Steven pointed to the same spot, Robbie hopped onto his bike and proceeded to run over the imaginary girl.

'See, there's no one here,' he said hopefully. Unfortunately Robbie didn't help. Steven became hysterical, crying and screaming because the girl wouldn't play with him, and because no one else could see that she was real. Caitlin tried explaining the girl was in his mind but he didn't believe her. So everyone ended up unhappy and frustrated.

Later on, after enrolling in one of my psychic development classes, Caitlin realised that Steven was actually psychic.

'He started seeing coloured circles around people. What he was seeing was their auras,' she told me. 'One day, when he was about six, my friend Brenda was over having coffee and Steven looked at her and said, "Mummy, her wheels aren't spinning right."'

When talking about 'wheels' Steven was describing Brenda's chakras or energy centres. These whirling energy centres do look like spinning wheels. Your body has seven main chakras, and each of these centres helps you to deal with different areas of life, such as your finances, sexuality, relating to others, speaking your mind, or connecting with nature, to name but a few applications.

At the time Caitlin had no idea what Steven was on about so she asked him what he meant.

Steven pointed to Brenda's chest, stomach and throat. 'Those wheels,' he said. He pointed to her throat chakra first and said, 'That one is going too far over there.' Although Steven didn't understand fully what he was seeing, he could see her throat chakra was out of alignment. This means that Brenda had an unresolved self-expression issue she needed to deal with. Then Steven pointed to her heart chakra. 'That one looks like it's got mud in it.' This indicated that Brenda was stuck in a no-win love situation. Then he pointed his finger down to Brenda's solar plexus chakra, just under the rib cage, and said, 'And this one is turned off.'

As Brenda struggled to hold back tears, Caitlin realised that Steven was undeniably right with what he was sensing. Brenda was going through a lot of emotional grief (heart chakra) with an ongoing dispute between her husband and son. She was feeling disempowered (solar plexus chakra) because neither of them was listening to her. Now it was showing up clearly in her chakras.

In the midst of all the drama there was a moment of humour as Robbie, who was also in the room, pointed out, 'I know how we can now make money, Mum. Let's start up a kids' psychic line!'

Being psychic, or having the sixth sense, is a gift. It means you have extrasensory perception, the ability to pick up information that the other five senses can't. Add clarity and insight to the mix and you have the perfect sensor that helps you get far more accurate impressions of what's going on in and around you. It also lets you do some pretty amazing things as well. Imagine being able to accurately predict the future or using your intuition to help your family and friends.

While some say that psychic ability is a gift that few people have, the truth is that all young children are psychic, even though it might not be apparent. Just because certain kids show more pronounced psychic tendencies than others, it doesn't mean that the rest aren't intuitive. The environment a child is in influences their ability to use their psychic talents. If they're in a noisy home where the TV is on 24/7, or where they never get the chance to be quiet or be outside in nature, their psychic gifts will tend to fade. This is because they are constantly being distracted, so they don't listen to their inner voice as much.

Children experience their sixth sense in their own unique way. Some *see* things such as a grandparent who is in spirit. Others intuitively *feel* what is going on around them, like picking up on your true emotions or the feeling of a situation. There are children who *hear* spirits talking to them. And there are kids who get a *sense*, or an inner knowing, about something without being told anything about it.

Given that so many children being born today are incredibly psychic, it's essential you have a deeper understanding of what's going on. This book will walk you through the beautiful world of the psychic child. It will give you an insight into why children *see*, *hear*, *feel* and *know* about things that lie beyond our everyday perception. By using the simple and practical tools provided here, you will be able to support and nurture your child's development. I'm sure you will also find that the process of unravelling the mystery behind their talent can be an inspiring and uplifting journey for you as well.

2

NEW KIDS ON THE BLOCK

The psychic child sees things differently to most adults and this is where tensions can arise. What is real to them might not seem real to you. And this is where your worlds separate—if you're not already working with your own psychic abilities then it can seem confusing and challenging to understand their exceptional perspective. So, what does it mean to be psychic? What kind of experiences is your child having? What adjustments do you need to make to help meet their needs and your own? Sometimes it seems like there are more questions than answers. And trying to sort reality from illusion can be difficult for concerned parents.

The key is to start by informing yourself about what goes on in their world—what a psychic child is and what they do. Once you understand what your child's psychic gift means and how it works, you'll feel confident enough to guide and nurture them.

How do you know if your child is psychic? Well, everyone is born psychic. However, some children are able to keep their psychic abilities open as they make the transition from childhood into adulthood. Others stop using their psychic abilities early on in life. It's not uncommon to find that psychic kids doubt they can be psychic. Also, just because a child's sixth sense isn't initially apparent doesn't mean that it's not playing out in their lives. It's easy to miss their intuition at work in inconsequential everyday things, like them knowing who's coming to visit before you announce it, or who's going to send the next message to them on Facebook. It's also easy to dismiss these small snippets of intuition as coincidence when they're not.

If you begin by assuming that your child does have psychic ability, it will help you to recognise their gift, even if it isn't fully developed. This is the first hurdle—breaking the belief that psychics are few and far between.

The next thing to recognise is that psychic children are *sensitive*. This doesn't necessarily mean that they are emotionally sensitive, although a lot are, but they are highly tuned into, and reactive to, their environment, just like six-year-old Krysta.

For months Krysta kept telling her mother, 'There is a little dark boy sitting on my bed.' Being young, she didn't know of another word to use to describe the Indigenous-looking boy.

Finally, one day her mother said, 'What does this little boy want?'

'He's scary. He wants me to go away,' replied Krysta.

'Why?'

'He won't say. He keeps telling me to get out . . . get out!'

Shortly after Krysta's mother took her to see a spiritual healer hoping for more than a healing—she needed answers.

The healer was also psychic and she used her ability to tune in on the spirit in Krysta's room.

'I'm seeing an image of an Indigenous boy. I'm being told that you are living on an old Indigenous sacred site,' she said. 'Did you know that?'

The next day Krysta's mother investigated the history of the Burns Bay Reserve in Lane Cove, Sydney. She discovered that it actually was once a sacred site. Indigenous people have a strong affinity to the land. They also believe that their ancestors walk among them. Sacred sites are very important to them, so it's easy to understand why the boy was trying to tell Krysta to get out.

The spiritual healer helped Krysta deal with her disturbing situation. She said Krysta had to close the doorway to the spirit world in her bedroom all by herself. Krysta's mother was a bit shocked by the suggestion. How could a little girl do that?

As it turns out, Krysta was up to the challenge, as these remarkable children are when you give them a voice.

'What can we do to help the little boy go?' asked her mother.

'What if I get my fairy wand and I send him magic white light fairy dust and tell him to go with his mummy?' said Krysta enthusiastically.

She did this and after that she never saw the boy again. Although she didn't necessarily understand what she was doing, Krysta was using the power of intention. She was determined to help this young boy in a loving way. You can use the power of intention too. If you focus your thoughts, or create a powerful loving statement of what is required, the energy of your words, and your actions, can produce wonderful results that benefit everyone.

Your child will really appreciate your involvement in situations like this. By seeking answers Krysta's mother was able to help support Krysta's unique view of life. This little girl has some valuable life skills. By helping her with them, her mother is supporting her daughter in numerous ways. You can do the same for yourself and for your child. If you don't know what to do, or you don't trust in your own sixth sense to help you deal with a situation like this, seek advice from someone recommended to you who you can trust. It will be a very special learning curve for everyone.

3

SENSESATIONAL

Krysta was opening up to her psychic abilities but she didn't understand it at the time. When your child is learning the lesson of what it is like to be psychic, they will have some fantastic growth spurts, which can be *sense*sational. And then there's bound to be the occasional hiccup as they develop their skills. It's perfectly reasonable for parents to want to know the ins and outs of being psychic. They often ask me, 'What happens to psychic children as they grow up?' and 'What kind of a psychic will they be?' because they worry that their kids may end up as the fringe-dwellers of a new frontier in consciousness and awareness. With support, however, these kids can lead very empowered, useful lives as adults. It doesn't mean that they can't be a brain surgeon, astronaut or best-selling writer. The important thing for parents is that they get up to speed. For most, it's back to the classroom to learn Psychic 101.

The first lesson is to understand what being psychic is and to explore the various types of psychic abilities your child might have. A psychic is someone who has the sixth sense, or extrasensory perception, and this gives them a heightened awareness, like sensitivity to energy, the ability to 'read' people's thoughts and feelings, or see what the future holds. But there is more than one way to psychically pick up information. The difference lies in how your sixth sense obtains its impressions. For example, your child could be a clairvoyant, clairaudient or clairsentient or they might be a medium or use telepathy. And they may have one or more of these sensory gifts.

If your child is clairvoyant it means that they *see* things. They get intuitive impressions through symbols, pictures or visions in their mind's eye. Sometimes they might even see an entire scene playing out in their mind as if they are watching a movie. A clairvoyant is a visual psychic.

The clairaudient child *hears* the voice of spirits talking to them. It might sound like the voice of a real person standing in the room, but there is no one there. Or, they may experience it as a voice talking inside their head. The voice might tell them about something that's about to happen or give them the answer to a question. This is their inner voice, the voice of their higher self, speaking to them. A clairaudient hears things psychically.

If your child is clairsentient it means that they *feel* things. They get impressions, or *sense* things, but quite often can't see auras or hear Spirit talking aloud. It plays out as an inner knowing that tells them what's going on with people or situations. So they can accurately sense what is going on in someone's aura, or they sense the presence of Spirit rather than see or hear it. They know how someone is feeling by picking up their vibe, or they might pick up on someone's pain by feeling the pain inside of their own body. A clairsentient is a feeling psychic.

A child with mediumship ability *communicates* with family and friends who are in spirit. They deliver messages of comfort and reassurance from our loved ones in spirit to let us know that they are okay and that they are watching over us. When this communication is opened, they get messages or intuitive impressions but they don't always see the spirit. Some mediums do get a vision in their mind's eye, which is the third-eye or the psychic chakra. A medium is a spiritual messenger.

Children who are telepathic are able to *tune* into your thoughts. They might not necessarily repeat what's on your mind verbatim, but they'll give you the overall gist of what you have been thinking. A telepath is a mind reader.

Why not spend a few moments reviewing your child's experiences? Which category do they fit into? Perhaps your child can work with a few of their psychic senses at the same time, such as being both clairaudient and clairsentient and therefore hearing and feeling things.

Either way, your child is one of a new breed of souls who are born equipped to work with their psychic ability. They need this skill because this generation has arrived in a rapidly changing world. They are geared up to deal with the problems associated with living in volatile and uncertain times, as long as we can nurture their gifts. Many have chosen to come into the world now to be agents of change. Being more switched on, or 'with it', than previous generations means that they can be visionaries.

You will have noticed that many of these children engage with the world differently because they are technologically savvy and have a highly refined sixth sense. Psychic kids are hardwired to absorb new levels of awareness and to push boundaries. Some of these exceptional children have come here to lead humanity to new heights.

Your psychic child has lot to contribute, especially when it comes to helping others reshape their perception of reality. Embracing your child's psychic sensitivity will make such a difference to their journey; and their journey will make such a difference to us all. They are our future.

4

EMBRACING YOUR PSYCHIC CHILD

Sweep away any lingering doubts you have about your child's extrasensory ability. There is nothing strange and unusual about being psychic. It is perfectly natural for them to use their sixth sense from an early age. You see, their intuition flows freely because they don't stop to analyse, or question, what they are picking up on psychically. Their intuitive mind is agile enough to capture details you miss because they are not hindered by a lifetime of conditioning that can box in perception. Innocence and openness let them welcome and accept the unexpected and their inquisitive and adventurous spirit helps them to explore realms that we often ignore. Things like getting premonitions or talking to invisible friends may seem to set them apart. But it's only a matter of perspective.

Because some children have such a noticeable gift, it's understandable why some parents compare their own kids to them. In doing so, they mistakenly undermine their own child's lovely talents. It's a real shame to discourage what your child senses. If you do, sooner or later they will believe that their psychic impressions were wrong, just like my sister Lena did.

'Do you remember when I was six how Dad used to threaten to take me to the old psychiatric hospital?' she asked me.

'Yes,' I said. I was only four at the time and although psychic myself, I couldn't see what Lena saw. This does not mean that one of us was wrong. Often, we tune into different aspects of the psychic world, or Spirit wants to be seen by one person and not by the other. At the time I didn't have a clue what was going on. 'Lena, you never told me why.'

'It was because he couldn't fathom why I was talking and laughing to myself when I was alone,' she said. 'He thought there was something wrong with me. He used to yell, "That's it, you lunatic, I'm taking you to the psychiatric hospital!" It used to frighten me because I really thought he was going to do it.'

'I thought he meant it too,' I said, grinning. It was so long ago and it's easy to smile at these things now.

'What he didn't seem to understand was that I was actually speaking to my "special friends". He couldn't see them; he only saw me laughing by myself as I walked towards the back of the yard. My friends used to lure me to play there so we could be alone together.'

'I wish you had told me. I would have loved to have played with them too. Did they come over every day?' I asked.

'No, they appeared randomly, whenever they felt like it. But when they were with me they would entertain me so much that I couldn't help but laugh. I loved talking with them because they seemed to understand me. They also liked me as I was.'

'I remember Mum used to get a little scared,' I mused.

'Yes, she couldn't understand it either,' said Lena. 'Every time I tried to explain my special friends to her or Dad, they got angry. It only made the situation worse. So I gave up trying.'

Eventually, Lena had to accept the fact that she had 'make believe' friends. My parents demanded that she stop talking to them. She wasn't even allowed to tell anyone about her special friends because they feared that our relatives would think she was mentally disturbed.

Now, looking back, Lena realises that her special friends were probably old souls or spirits that had not passed over. They would come and play with her because she was open to them. She believed in them and felt that they were real. It was curious that they only appeared to her when she was alone. Lena now thinks this was because we belonged to a large family of five kids.

'They didn't appear because I was a lonely child but because I could communicate with them. I wasn't frightened to talk and play with them.'

Lena explained her special friends were a brother and sister, around her age, named Jack and Annie. 'They were always laughing and into mischief and delighted in making fun of Mum and Dad's fears. We used to run into the backyard and play. Sometimes they'd ask me to play with them in the farm paddocks. They even talked me into playing with them at the back of our neighbour's properties, hiding in spots where no one could see me. Jack and Annie were very secretive about themselves but, being a kid, I didn't ask them too many questions. I just accepted them as they were.'

'Why do you think they chose you?' I asked.

'I don't know,' she said, shrugging. 'I think they wanted to feel like they belonged. I sensed they were lost and looking for their family and that's why they took me away from the house to play in the paddocks. Jack and Annie kept asking me to help look for something. I thought it was only a game and didn't quite understand but I think they needed to find their lost family. I didn't know why they couldn't just come and live with us.'

Without question, Lena accepted the fact that the reason only she, and no one else, could see them was because Jack and Annie were her special friends.

'I was happy. It made me feel special to have them and that I didn't have to share them with the other kids,' she said. 'Remember how I used to have to share everything with you?'

'Yes. So it would have been hard having to let go of Jack and Annie,' I empathised.

'It was, but Dad's threats to send me away scared me so much that I did what he ordered me to do. I told them they had to go and find their family alone. They couldn't understand why, because they were kids too, and they didn't realise how the idea of being sent to the psychiatric hospital overwhelmed me. Eventually, Jack and Annie seemed to accept this fact. They were crying. I was terribly sad when they left. It felt like I had lost a part of me.'

'Do you still think about them?' I asked. 'Did you ever think about what might have happened to them?'

'It's funny, I've never thought of myself as being psychic,' Lena said, 'but now that I think about it, I do sense Jack and Annie around me from time to time. I usually feel them around me when I'm feeling sad and alone. I don't believe they are still lost, I think Jack and Annie found their family eventually and they're not stuck anymore. Now they choose to come across from the spirit world and visit me. They don't actually talk to me but I get glimpses of them. When they are around I feel a sense of calm, as if they are my guardian angels who are spending some time with a little girl who showed them some kindness once.'

So-called 'imaginary friends' are important to psychic children. As Lena said, 'Jack and Annie were a part of my life. They will always hold a special place in my heart.'

All too often children are talked into closing off their psychic abilities. By closing off, they begin to ignore what they are sensing. Also, the age of seven, when the logical mind kicks in, can be a turning point for some kids. They seem to forgo their psychic self and start spending more time in their logical mind. Did you know that this happens around the same time that the fontanelle at the top of the skull closes up? It's quite symbolic because the fontanelle is located in the same spot as the crown chakra. The crown chakra is the wisdom chakra, a centre of consciousness that helps you to connect to all things. Very often, by the time a child reaches seven this chakra isn't as open as it used to be because they are usually educated to start favouring critical thinking in the Western schooling system. But it doesn't have to be this way. By embracing your psychic child and giving them the guidance and assistance they need, you can help them remain psychically open so they can shine.

Children need to feel supported in what they see and sense and, as a parent, you are their most important guide. They trust you. If you tell them to stop playing with these imaginary friends, it can make them sad but also make them distrust their sense of reality.

If you feel like you have already discouraged your child from believing in their spirit friends, why not encourage them to believe in them again? Why not sit down at the table with them and get them to draw what their special friends look like? Perhaps they can draw where they are from, or the story of their lives. Then you can discuss the pictures with them and help them with any of your own intuitive insights on their special friends.

5

I SPY WITH MY LITTLE EYE

Lena was using both her clairvoyant (seeing) and clair-audient (hearing) abilities when she was playing with Jack and Annie. However, not all kids can hear Spirit. Some specialise in one skill alone, like clairvoyance. Has your child ever seen snap-shots of the future? Many kids make great clairvoyants because they easily receive visual impressions in their mind's eye. This psychic sensor gives them the ability to tap into the past, *see clearly* what is really going on in the moment, and look into the future. And they are often incredibly accurate! Sometimes it makes you wonder, 'How could they know that?'

Being clairvoyant can be very comforting to them because they know what to expect. This means that they can be prepared for, and very accepting of, unfolding events. It is a beautiful gift to have, and one that they can use to help others.

Michael started getting psychic impressions when he was eleven. He correctly predicted the arrival date of his sister, who was born weeks before the due date. Now, at fifteen, he has his own tarot deck and the word on the street is that he is a gifted psychic. His 'career' kickstarted in November 2010 when his mother took him to the reiki healing group she was involved in.

'I knew he was a natural healer because at four he was able to clear my migraines,' his mother told me. 'I never taught him any techniques; he just intuitively knew what to do. Everyone in the reiki group was drawn to him and whenever he assisted others in healings, he started getting visions of what was happening. Then one day he started giving one-card tarot readings to strangers, and he was spot-on,' she said. 'It wasn't a matter of hit or miss, he was always right.'

A few days later, while his mother was on the phone to a friend who was experiencing some difficulties, she called out, 'Michael, will you do a reading for Karen?'

Michael was happy to do it because he enjoys working with his psychic abilities. He tuned in and immediately said that Karen was having relationship problems. 'Oh, and she's planning a trip overseas—to England.'

'That was the first I'd heard of her plans,' his mother said. 'And it turns out Michael's reading was correct.'

Suddenly, people were sending SMS messages to her asking if Michael could do telephone psychic readings for them. A clairvoyant can read for people sitting in front of them but they're equally capable of doing long-distance readings. This means that they can do an accurate reading for someone living halfway across the world. Location doesn't matter because your clairvoyant channel is multidimensional; time and space don't place restrictions on your ability.

Michael makes a point of asking them not to tell him anything, just to think about their issues. While they are doing this, he deals the tarot. He doesn't actually follow the literal interpretation of the cards; he goes with the images and pictures that pop into his head, and gets a feeling for what is going on. The tarot cards give his gift a focus.

On another occasion Michael got a call from a teenage girl. He tuned in and kept telling her, 'Your sister is trying to speak to you. Why aren't you listening? She is standing next to you and is saying something about you having to believe in Spirit.'

'But my sister is dead,' the girl said.

Michael then described her sister's personality and what she looked like. He was clearly connecting to her sister's spirit.

I was intrigued by Michael's story and, when his mother asked me if I would like a reading from Michael, I loved the idea. Without telling him anything, I focused on my investment property, which is currently being renovated so I can put it on the market in a few weeks.

'I'm seeing a financial matter around you that is taking up a lot of time,' he began. 'There are changes to do with money and you haven't got full control yet because it involves other people and things are stalling. You feel responsible for these other people so it's affecting you financially. It is a burden to you.'

He was right. My son Tristan and his friends have been renting my house for several months but now they are going to have to find a new place to live. The renovation has been a burden because it's running behind schedule. And trying to help my son find a new place, as well as managing the renovations, while running my business, is a little exhausting. Another interesting point was that Michael also saw me standing by Stonehenge. I am actually planning a trip to the Pyramids and Stonehenge with a group of students for 2012.

There are many children like Michael who have wonderful gifts to offer the world when they are nurtured, guided and protected.

If your child is starting to show some clairvoyant abilities, help them understand how clairvoyance works through visions and pictures. Ask them to look at the symbols that appear in their mind and what they mean to them. If they don't understand them, perhaps you can offer a few interpretations so they slowly get the hang of decoding the symbols and pictures they see psychically. If you don't trust in your psychic abilities to decode the symbols you can always look up their meaning on the internet. Another alternative is to grab a good dream interpretation book. These books explain the meaning of hundreds of symbols. Eventually, kids will develop their own interpretation system. But, in the meantime, they may need your help and guidance. For example, if they have a vision of you stepping on a plane and see a tree with no leaves and snow on the ground, it could mean that you will be travelling during winter. If they see an enormous wave coming towards you, it can mean that you are feeling emotionally overwhelmed. When you make the time to engage with their world, you are a great comfort to them, as their special talents begin to unfold.

6

THEY TOLD ME SO

It is important to understand how clairvoyance works through pictures and symbols, but it is equally important to stay open to the different kinds of senses your child can work with. Lately there has been a groundswell of interest in mediumship and, as a result, a lot of people pigeonhole this as the only true psychic ability. Nothing could be further from the truth. Psychic abilities are expressed through a number of different modalities. It is wise to remember this and keep an open mind when your child expresses a different kind of intuition.

One area of intuition that is largely overlooked is the ability to communicate with nature. Kids have an affinity with the natural kingdom but how often do you pay attention when they start talking about seeing fairies in the garden? It's only their playful imagination, right? Well, not always. You see, nature is also full of consciousness. Every living thing you see around you has a spirit—trees, plants, animals—and they all have a story to tell.

Several years ago my ex-husband Stephen took our son Tristan away to spend quality time together to strengthen the father–son bond. But he also had another agenda. He wanted to provide Tristan with a sort of 'rite of passage' into his spiritual heritage by learning to meditate and open his psychic ability further. Tristan has always been psychic but it's not a gift he felt comfortable with while growing up because, like many other sensitive souls, he often absorbed too much of other people's stuff. He became reluctant to work with his psychic ability until we taught him how to create a healthy boundary between his own energies and everyone else's. Now he was ready.

They headed to the tranquil mountains that fringe the hinterland of the far north coast of New South Wales. Getting away from the buzz of city life was just what they needed in order to meditate and 'open up' to whatever spiritual experience came their way. Stephen and Tristan decided to meditate in the heart of the breathtaking subtropical rainforest. With sunlight breaking through the tall canopies into bright beams that flooded the rich undergrowth, and the sound of running water from a crystal-clear stream, they sat cross-legged and meditated. Shortly afterwards Stephen asked Tristan to select and stand by a tree while intuitively tuning into what the tree was seeing and feeling. Having never done anything like this before, Tristan gave his father a quizzical look.

'Just try it,' Stephen suggested. 'It doesn't matter if you get nothing; just stay open to the experience.'

'I like this one,' said Tristan, standing in front of a tree with rich green foliage and twisted roots that rose from the ground like arteries.

'Okay, put your hands on the trunk and ask the tree permission to talk with it and then listen to its story.'

Trees, like people, have a story to tell. We see, hear and feel things and so do trees. They experience it differently to us but their experience is still valid. And Indigenous people, who have a strong affinity to the land, would probably agree with me.

Tristan placed his hands on the trunk and closed his eyes and tuned in. Several minutes later he started crying and pulled his hands away from the tree.

'What's wrong?' asked his father.

'This tree is sad,' replied Tristan. 'It's crying because it's so distressed.'

'Why is it distressed?'

'Because the other trees are dying,' he said tearfully. 'They're being cut down and this tree is sad for them but also worried that it's going to be cut down too.'

Stephen looked around. He couldn't see or hear any logging operations and he was sure he didn't see any on the drive into the forest.

'What can I do to help the trees?' asked Tristan, his maturity surprising his father.

Stephen explained how he could visualise a strong ray of yellow light coming through him and out of his solar plexus chakra (our manifestation chakra) and send it to all the trees in the area. He then told him to send out a ray of electric blue light to give them healing, followed by a rich pink light to give them unconditional love. He also suggested calling on angels to help them deal with the trauma. Tristan did this and immediately felt much more hopeful because he knew he was doing all he could to alleviate their distress.

Afterwards they left the forest and about ten minutes into the drive back to the coast where they were staying, they were shocked to see a logging operation. Tristan's psychic ability had accurately picked up what the tree was experiencing. Loggers were already cutting down trees in the area and the trees were trying to warn each other.

When I recounted this story to a few people, they were sceptical, yet research has shown that plants do actually communicate with each other. They communicate telepathically through chemical messages known as pheromones. In an experiment using tomato plants, which were infested with pests, researchers discovered that the distressed plants not only managed to release a toxin to kill the pests, but they were also sending out additional chemical messages to warn surrounding plants. Some might argue that this is a purely physical response by plants. Any person open to energy will tell you that trees and plants are also energetic beings. Sure, they may be sentient forms of consciousness, and they have a different form of consciousness to humans, but nevertheless they have a spirit essence as well.

There is a broad scope to kids' psychic abilities. Even though your child's gift might not seem as impressive as seeing spirits or picking winning Lotto numbers, they might have a talent for intuitively communicating with nature, and knowing what other living beings need. Given these difficult times of environmental chaos, having a generation that can tune in and tell us what nature needs for sustainability is definitely something to look forward to.

7

TEN LITTLE FINGERS

Another ability that is often overlooked is children's intuitive healing abilities. They might not understand how the body works or the nature of illness but that does not mean they can't heal others. Their tiny fingers can hold incredible healing energies! I feel this stems from their innocence and their desire to help. The secret to their talent is simply this — it's all in their intention. Whatever their heart and soul injects into their energies is amplified tremendously and can make for some beautiful healing.

Only the other day Araceli was telling me how her five-year-old son Nathan saw her lying on the lounge. He asked her what was wrong and she explained that she had a headache. He instinctively knew what he had to do. Placing his hands across her head, he said brightly, 'I make you all better?'

Araceli, who is an energy healer, mustered a smile, thinking he was going to rub her temples, but instead he kept his hands firmly pressed against her head and was silent. She felt a strong, warm energy coming out from his tiny fingers that seeped into her head.

'I was so surprised,' she admitted. 'It was the first time he ever tried something like this and my headache went away in minutes. When I told him I felt better, he smiled like the Cheshire cat, so proud of himself.'

She asked him to explain what he was thinking about during the healing session. Nathan didn't understand the mechanics of what he was doing, he was simply following what he felt was right, which was thinking thoughts about her feeling better.

Spiritual healing and reiki use energy to facilitate wellness. They also complement traditional medicine because they are holistic. The secret of this kind of healing lies in the power of clear intention. Illness and disease stem from disharmony within the aura. When your energies become stagnant and blocked, or vibrate at a lower frequency, you will feel unwell. It is your soul's way of saying, 'Look within, what is it that you need to deal with? What needs to be emotionally or psychologically fixed or released from your inner self?'

By stating a clear intention you imbue universal energies with a directive and this generates a power circuit through your aura that can remove discordant frequencies from your energies. It restores balance by freeing up blocked energies you are holding on to. That's what makes this kind of healing so effective — the logical mind doesn't butt in to disrupt the focus. Araceli added, 'Nathan didn't use any healing techniques, he wouldn't know about these kinds of things, he just kept thinking about the pain leaving me and it did.'

Even if your child only performs simple little healing tasks, such as putting their love and positive thoughts into hugs, through their fingers or just into caring words, they can make you feel better. Then there are children who are born healers, kids whose soul path will take them on the healer's journey later on in life.

Both my psychic kids are natural healers but they express it in different ways. Chiara, who is now sixteen years old, has always done it through looking out for the welfare of others, like taking care of younger kids at school who were feeling lost or lonely. Or she's played 'counsellor' by listening to her friends and making them feel better with soothing words and sage advice. Tristan, who is twenty years old, was born to work more on people's energy system, like their aura and chakras. Your soul is your aura; it is the part of you that holds your essence and your true light. Your aura also contains seven main chakras. A chakra is a spinning vortex of energy that holds a seat of consciousness. The chakras have two functions. The first is physiological—they transmute universal and earth energy for use by the body; the second is spiritual—they act as a doorway to higher consciousness. When he tunes into a chakra Tristan can psychically pick up what has been happening in someone's life.

Recently, Tristan stepped up to the mark and put his healing skills to work. After years of being told by his spirit guides that he is here to protect and heal others, he got the opportunity. His client? Actually, it was his father. My ex-husband Stephen had a stroke even though he is only in his forties.

The call came late on a Saturday night and before Chiara and I jumped into the car she turned to me and said, 'I can help him get well. You know how I can absorb other people's emotions, well, can't I do the same thing and absorb all of his pain and get rid of his illness? That will help Daddy.'

It was a beautiful offer but not a practical one; it's never wise to take someone's pain into your own energy system. There are better ways to heal them and I explained this to her.

On the way to the hospital Tristan tuned in and got a psychic vision of what Stephen was doing just prior to having the stroke.

'He was having a glass of red wine and thinking about taking a drive somewhere, I think it was the beach,' he told me.

Later, when we were by his bedside, Stephen was able to confirm Tristan's insight. We were lucky that Stephen was awake despite the haemorrhagic stroke that was pouring blood into the part of the brain that rules his speech. He alternated between lucid then incoherent moments but the message got through and it was important for Tristan to hear his father validating what he saw while tuning in. Given a confidence boost that his psychic abilities were switched on, Tristan focused on his father and asked his guides, 'Will he survive?'

Tristan got the message loud and clear in his third eye: 'Yes, he will.'

Three days later we visited Stephen in the intensive care unit so I could do further spiritual healing on him. This time Tristan offered to assist in the healing. This is a huge step; helping heal your own father is a daunting task but Tristan really wanted to help.

I gave him instructions on what energy to send to his father's chakras and other tips on working with the aura and he set about doing it. He was in his element, although at times he looked a little uncertain.

When we finished a staff member came over to collect Stephen to deliver him to radiology. He was a slim Indian man in his early fifties with a broad smile and caring energy.

'Modern medicine is good, it is needed,' he said. 'But what you are doing is also good. It is good for the soul.'

We had been so involved in the healing we didn't notice him watching us. He drew closer until he stood at the foot of the bed.

'You must believe in what you do, young man,' he advised. Clearly the man was energy aware and quite intuitive himself.

'Thanks,' replied Tristan. He acknowledged there were moments when he waivered during the healing session. But that is also understandable. It was all so new to him and he wanted to make sure that everything he was doing was right because his father was still not out of danger.

I was incredibly proud of Tristan for pushing past his comfort zone and I was impressed that the hospital had an open-minded staff member who understood the value of energetic healing. Stephen made a rapid recovery. Going through this experience gave Tristan a newfound confidence in another psychic ability he had—the ability to work with energy to help heal others. The uplifting love he experienced while healing his father was definitely worth pushing his psychic ability by stepping into the world of energy healing.

Tristan understands that he is still on a steep learning curve, that being psychic is a lifelong journey into self-discovery. With every step he takes Tristan knows he is unwrapping a new level of awareness and broadening his perceptual boundary. Some people climb the highest mountain so they can stand on the summit with arms stretched open wide and marvel at the breathtaking beauty. In this dazzling moment they realise how different the world below them is. Some people climb a different summit—a perceptual summit that opens up a completely new breathtaking world.

8

POPPY'S HERE

Your psychic child will surprise you with their spontaneous insights which can happen anytime, anywhere. It is one of their most endearing qualities. You have probably already noticed they're very responsive to what's going on around them and don't always question it, especially if it's something 'out there'. This can be anything from seeing the spirit of a loved one walking around the house, to what's going to happen to you next week. Young children will take psychic impressions on board and run with them.

Fiona's new bookshelf arrived a few days after she moved into her house. While her two-year-old daughter Callie was sleeping, Fiona grabbed the opportunity to pull out a box of precious ornaments from storage and began placing them on the bookshelf. She put an unattractive, but sentimental, 'Hole In One' golf trophy belonging to her deceased father at the back of the shelf, behind some family photos. The trophy had been in storage for eighteen months.

Later on in the day Fiona walked into the family room and noticed Callie talking to herself and staring up at the ceiling.

'Who are you talking to?' Fiona asked.

'Poppy,' she said. Callie had never met her grandfather. He died five years before she was born.

'What does Poppy look like?' questioned Fiona.

'He has hair on his face, Mummy,' she replied, still looking up at the ceiling.

'What colour is it?'

'It's orange and has silver stripes,' she said immediately.

Fiona quickly scanned the assortment of family pictures on the bookshelf. The only photos of her father were in black and white, or taken when he was younger and had a dark beard. There was no way Callie could know his beard had turned reddish and grey as he aged.

'What is he wearing?' she inquired.

'He's got a small red lion on the top of his shirt,' replied Callie.

This detail caught Fiona's attention. Her father always wore a Holden shirt with a red lion motif on the front when he played golf.

'Poppy says he likes having his trophy out,' said Callie, smiling.

Fiona was blown away by that bit. Callie had never seen the trophy before; she didn't even know what a trophy was. Fiona didn't think Callie could even see it, given her height and where it was placed. This small piece of information was enough to validate what Callie was saying. She couldn't have made up these details.

'Where do you see Poppy?' asked Fiona. 'Point to him for me.'

'He's floating, up there,' Callie said, pointing to the space between the bookshelf and the ceiling. 'Can you see him? He's smiling at me, Mummy, and doing that thing with his eye.'

Callie tried to mimic the wink that she saw Poppy doing. It was his personal calling card. When Fiona was growing up, he would express his pleasure in her behaviour by smiling and giving her an exaggerated wink with his right eye.

Fiona felt a warm, loving feeling wash over her. Her dad's visit to her new home suggested he was happy with the direction she was taking with her life. Even though Fiona couldn't see her father's spirit, she knew Callie was telling her the truth. Fiona is a schoolteacher and is sensible, grounded and sceptical. While she is the 'I'll believe it when I see it' type of person, she is also open-minded and believes in spirits.

'Callie described Dad perfectly,' Fiona told me. 'And how could she know how important that trophy was to him? I knew this wasn't an imaginary friend. I know this sort of stuff can happen.'

Fiona recalled one psychic experience she had when she first met her ex-husband Wayne's family. 'I saw his grandfather's spirit and I was wondering why the family weren't introducing me to the man standing in a doorway off the hall. And I couldn't understand why he didn't come into the room to join us. Wayne's mother came up to me and asked, "What are you looking at?" Not wanting to sound crazy, I said nothing.'

But when she persisted Fiona finally said, 'The old man.'

'What does he look like?' asked Wayne's mother.

'Mid height, thin, hunched shoulders, blue uniform, bushy eyebrows,' replied Fiona. 'Oh, yes, he's also frowning.' Then he disappeared.

'Yes, that'll be him,' Wayne's mother told Fiona. 'That's my father.'

She walked into the kitchen and returned with a photo, which Fiona immediately recognised as the man she had seen.

'That was a real eye-opener,' she admitted.

Since Fiona had this kind of experience herself, she was definitely open to listening to Callie. Little Callie is lucky to have this loving support. Sadly, many parents dismiss these kinds of situations because they're unnerved or because they're trying to find a logical explanation. This can be hurtful, shaming or confusing for a young child.

Perhaps you could meet your child halfway by learning how to finetune your own sixth sense? This way you can both be on the same page.

All you need to do is to reawaken what lies dormant within you. You had psychic abilities as an infant, but one day you stopped using these abilities and started relying on the senses of taste, touch, sight, sound and smell to guide you instead. Why did this happen? There are a lot of reasons why you can end up losing touch with your psychic ability. It could have been because it was never encouraged by your parents. Or perhaps you were educated to favour logic over intuition? Now, you have the opportunity to do something about it. You can start to stimulate your psychic abilities by trusting in your gut feelings. You may just be surprised at what happens.

9

I KNEW IT!

You might not think your child is especially psychic but they probably get great hunches. A hunch is a gut feeling about something. You might not understand the impressions you're getting, but the feeling says, 'Hey, pay attention'. Hunches can be premonitions. A premonition is a forewarning—a sense of knowing what is going to unfold before it actually does. Kids get them all the time without knowing that they're actually having one because they don't know how to label this kind of experience.

If you have ever had a premonition, you too may have found it hard understanding it at the time because they're not always easy to identify. Instead of following your hunch you end up getting stuck in an internal dialogue with yourself. 'Is it wishful thinking? Perhaps I read it somewhere? Maybe my imagination is getting the better of me?' And not all premonitions stem from a hunch, vision or feeling; sometimes they happen in your dreams. Premonitions aren't always easy to interpret because they might come when you least expect it.

I believe that if you stay open to your premonitions, and encourage your child to tune into theirs, then some truly wonderful things can happen as a result of listening to them. What I love about premonitions is that I get to see a snapshot of what the future holds and this gives me a sense of comfort because I can make the most of it. You and your child can gain a sense of security that comes with knowing.

Last November, twelve-year-old Stella got a premonition in a dream where she saw herself walking down the driveway of her aunt's house. Then the phone rang and she heard her mother's voice on the other end saying, 'Nan's just passed away.'

The following night Stella started dreaming about snakes. 'Small snakes were dancing around a tree in a circle,' she told me. 'And I knew this represented us six kids and that Nanna had just passed away.' When I pressed her on how she knew this, Stella said she didn't know how, she just *knew*.

Stella had no idea why she was having these dreams but they persisted, the same dream occurring nightly. 'The snakes were writhing and dancing on their tails around the tree. Over the weeks the dream got clearer, I could see faces, and more information was coming to light,' she explained.

'Then one night I had the same dream about Nan again, the one where I was walking down the driveway when the phone rang with the news of her death.' At the time Stella couldn't understand why she felt this dream was 'real', as opposed to other dreams that are a clearing house for our subconscious, or us seeking to experience what we 'dream of'. She just knew this dream felt strange and made her feel uneasy.

A few weeks later Stella's aunt invited the kids to holiday at her place by the beach. 'One day, while we were at the beach, Aunty Marg wanted us kids to go and visit Nanna at the retirement home. I refused to go as I knew she would soon die.' Again Stella didn't know why she felt that this was true, she just knew it. So instead of going with her aunt and the other kids to visit their nan, Stella chose to stay at the beach.

'They came back to the beach after visiting Nan and Aunty Marg kept saying, "Come on, hurry up, we have to go back home." When we got there, we all got out of the car, and I was walking down the driveway, just like I was in my dream. It felt really weird, I was living my dream. Then the phone rang and we got the news that Nanna had just passed away.'

Stella started crying because she felt that she'd let everyone down. 'I thought that if I had told people about my dream, Nanna would still be alive.'

This experience frightened Stella. Perhaps your child has had a similar experience, a premonition that has come true but it's scared them because they saw something before it actually happened? Stella tried to stop having these kinds of dreams and visions but she couldn't. Unfortunately, at the time her mother didn't understand the nature of dreams and premonitions so she wasn't able to soothe Stella.

Premonition dreams can form the basis for a later déjà vu experience. Déjà vu is the sense of having previously experienced something even though you know you haven't. Chiara's déjà vu moment happened when she was eight years old. She'd dreamt that she was running late for school. When she arrived she found a substitute teacher, who had long blonde hair and green eyes, taking the class. She wasn't one of the regular substitute teachers but she seemed really nice. The teacher asked the kids to do drawings. Chiara decided to draw an alien with an upside-down purple triangle head.

The next day Chiara arrived late to school and walked into class and saw they had a blonde substitute teacher. She thought she looked vaguely familiar but couldn't put her finger on why. Later on in the day, the teacher asked the class to do a drawing. Chiara drew an alien with a circular head but decided she didn't like the way it looked. She rubbed it out and drew an upside-down purple triangle head. It was in that exact moment that she realised, 'Hang on a minute, haven't I done this before?'

A friend's daughter, Serena, dreamt about a house on the hill on a cliff side. It was a white mansion surrounded by a windswept coastal garden.

More than a year later, they were in the car with her dad driving them to a holiday place where they had never been. Serena saw the white mansion on the cliff side and instinctively knew she had seen the house before but couldn't remember where. Suddenly she yelled out to her dad, 'Stop the car, I know this house.'

He slowed down.

'I know this house,' Serena repeated.

While this was happening a man in another car overtook them and about forty seconds later he had a collision with an oncoming car.

Serena's déjà vu moment saved them from having an accident.

Remember, some dreams are prophetic; you've just taken a peek into the future but you don't realise it when you wake up, and we tend to forget most of our dreams. So, as you're going through the motions of an experience and you're getting that uncanny sense of 'I've been here before', it's very likely that you have. It goes to show how our reality does operate on so many unique levels.

Premonition dreams are psychic dreams. They draw your attention to a future event that will unfold. Some premonition dreams empower you to change an event before it happens. For example, if you dreamt that Uncle Charlie fell down the stairs on Sunday night and broke his leg, you can suggest that he take extra care on that particular night especially when he is on the stairs and the accident might be avoided. However, some premonition dreams are about fated events that need to play out because of karma. In these cases you might not be able to control the outcome, but perhaps you were never meant to. Instead the dream gives you the opportunity to prepare yourself and shows how to deal with it, so you can still feel empowered even though you cannot control the outcome of the event itself.

10
DREAM WEAVER

A premonition dream is one example of the types of dreams children have. Others include release, lesson/repeat, teaching, nightmares and answer dreams. Whichever way you look at it, dreams have a purpose. This might sound crazy, especially since they are often abstract, surreal and even downright weird. The truth is that dreams open a window to the soul. Their purpose is to make you aware of what is really going on inside your unconscious mind and soul. Would you like to open that window? See what is really going on in your child's inner realm?

I feel it is important to pay attention to their dreams because it does show you that being psychic is natural, and it plays out in simple ways in our everyday life.

One morning four-year-old Jack ran into Cherie's bedroom and said, 'Aunty Nez is coming over today!'

Cherie responded, 'No, I don't think so, mate.'

'Yes, she is,' he replied determinedly. 'She told me in my dreams that she was coming today.'

Cherie didn't think much of it until an hour later when her sister Nez dropped in unexpectedly (well, at least Jack expected her!) and said that last night when she was in bed she was thinking it had been a while since she'd seen the children and thought she should visit in the morning.

'Now Jack regularly tells me things like, "Oh, that's Nanny on the phone," and two seconds later the phone rings!' Cherie told me. And Jack is always right. Sceptics might argue that Jack is guessing since he knows his grandmother rings often, but Jack knows the phone is going to ring before it does, and also identifies each person who is calling.

It is not something you have to do daily but it would be wise to occasionally check in with your child and ask, 'What did you dream about last night?' Kids are open and spontaneous but there are times when they cannot articulate what they are feeling inside, what has ruffled their feathers, what is niggling at them. Children are not equipped to analyse every aspect of their lives so when certain problems arise they may not be able to correctly identify what it is or why it's happening. It could be simple everyday issues like having problems with other kids at preschool, or feeling overwhelmed by homework or confused about what is happening at home. Since they cannot put their finger on what is simmering under the surface of their awareness, how can they express what is really going on?

So, problems get swept under the carpet and issues are left unattended simply because kids cannot identify, or effectively communicate, their concerns. And that is such a pity when dreams can act as a link between your child's inner and outer world. Dreams can put you in the know.

If you want to get a glimpse of what your child's true soul urge and desires are, why not look into their dreams?

Dreams will surrender their secrets. The key to unlocking this treasure trove of insights is to understand dreams and how to interpret them. Both you and your child will reap the benefits if you spend a few minutes analysing a dream.

A dream is a message from the inner you. Initially, when you fall asleep you might spend time sorting through, and releasing, events from the day. The important stuff is filed away in the 'must need' box while everything else you experience is stored in the memory box. Once this is done, then real dreaming kicks in and this deeper stage of dreaming is where the messages start flowing.

Dreams generated from the unconscious mind stem from issues that have been bugging your child which have been pushed into the 'too hard to handle' basket by the conscious mind. Like adults, kids today have very busy lives full of distraction so they don't get much 'me time' to sort through what experiences they need to hold on to, which emotions to let go of and how to resolve confusing situations. So the unconscious mind brings them to their attention while they are sleeping.

For example, if your child dreams that they are standing by the ocean and a huge tsunami is coming straight at them but breaks just before it reaches their feet, it is a message from the subconscious that they are feeling emotionally overwhelmed. But, since the wave does break and does not take them under, it suggests that they are able to cope with it. You can ask them how they are feeling about things to pinpoint which part of their life is giving them emotional grief, then counsel them to reassure them that they will be okay. Their subconscious is trying to release these bottled-up emotions.

Dreams help children play out unresolved issues and find answers or resolution. Through dreams they have the perfect opportunity to get some much-needed emotional healing, even if they do not realise that this is what is actually happening. The unconscious mind can release deep pent-up fears through the dream state so your child does not have to hold on to them. Nightmares are one way the unconscious mind tries to help them confront uncomfortable thoughts and feelings and repressed fears. It does this through symbols.

Symbols are the language of the soul. We think in pictures so it is no surprise that we dream in pictures. These pictures are symbols that can help you reconstruct an experience stored as a long-term memory that needs to be released. Triggering the original sensations of any unresolved issue gives you the opportunity to review the experience in a non-threatening dream-state environment so you can facilitate emotional repair.

Another important function of dreams is that they serve as a live broadcast from the soul, helping your child discover new ideas and inspiration—literally how to reach their 'dreams'. These kinds of dreams help them get in touch with their true desire and offer hope. Discussing these dreams with your child will enrich you both.

The secret to understanding dreams is simple. Decode the symbols. Initially you might find decoding difficult. After all, how do you make sense of a dream where your child is 'flying high in the clear blue sky wearing a purple panda suit'? Or, your child hits you with, 'I was swimming with dolphins in a swimming pool without water!'

An easy way is to do this:

Symbol	Interpretation	Emotion
Flying	Rising above limits	Uplifting
Clear blue sky	Expansive, no interruptions from clouds	Feeling free
Purple	Colour of the crown chakra Represents Spirit, connection to all things, higher consciousness	Peaceful
Panda	Soft, childlike qualities	Safe and uncomplicated

Write down the symbol then ask your child to tell you what they think the symbol means. If they cannot interpret the symbol ask them to draw the symbol and encourage them to talk about it. As they are sharing their dream, let your intuition guide you to help interpret the meaning of each symbol.

It is important to associate a symbol with an emotion. How your child feels about each symbol will help you gain a deeper understanding of the dream. Ask your child, 'How did you feel swimming with the dolphins even though there wasn't any water?' or, 'What do you think of when you think about dolphins?'

Now all you have to do is string together the symbols, interpretation and emotions and you will get the answer to what the dream means.

Keeping this line of communication open with your child by regularly checking in on their dreams will help you help them deal with issues and even map out aspects of their future.

11

ONCE UPON A TIME

One of the most endearing things about kids is their openness, which is probably why they are really good at accessing hidden parts of themselves. They can intuitively touch base with hidden memories of their past lives.

Have you ever had a fascination for a certain country, culture or period in time? Chances are you had a past life there. What kind of past lives do you think your child has had? Were they a soldier, artist or inventor? If they were, what does it have to do with this current life?

A lot, actually, because past-life memories are brought forward and since psychic kids are old souls, they have a lot of past-life memories playing out in their cellular memory. Working with past lives can help you understand their personality traits, the kind of things that keep happening to them and why they have some deep-seated fears that make no sense. For example, they might fear dogs though they have never been bitten by one or they may be the 'head in the clouds' type although both parents are grounded. It also helps you understand their soul karma. This is the life lessons you need to experience in this life that are based on the actions taken in previous lives.

Karma is the law of cause and effect. This means everything you do has consequences—you're either creating new karma or clearing out old karma through your thoughts, feelings and actions. I like to call karma 'the equaliser' because it is energy trying to find balance. If the scales are lopsided, you still have karma to deal with, which means having to make adjustments in your thinking, feeling and actions in order to balance the karmic energy. Sometimes, you are the one creating new karma; at other times you may be balancing karma from your past-life deeds.

It is these past-life deeds that create the karma that determines your child's gifts and challenges this time around. Having an insight into your child's karmic game plan can help you to better understand their nature. This information can help you help them to overcome restrictive patterns and open up to their true potential. It's certainly worth looking into, especially if your little psychic child has already started giving you titbits about their past lives themselves.

You may have heard of the famous story of Shanti Devi.[1] At four Shanti started talking about her 'husband' and her 'children'. By six she talked about her life in the town of Mathura with her husband, who was fair-skinned, had a big wart on his left cheek and wore reading glasses. She said his favourite dishes were stuffed potato parathas and pumpkin squash. Shanti insisted that his home was located in front of the Dwarkadhish temple, and there was a well in the courtyard of their house where she used to take her bath. Shanti called herself Ludgi and was able to give an account of the medical procedures conducted on her before her death after childbirth. Her knowledge of the procedures amazed her local doctor.

For years the girl begged her family to take her to her 'home' but they did not know what to do. Finally, at age nine, she revealed to her cousin that her husband's name was Pandit Kedarnath Chaube. Her cousin wrote to Kedarnath who confirmed Shanti's claims. One day Kedarnath, his new wife and Ludgi's son Navneet Lal decided to visit the girl. She cried at the sight of her son from her former life.

After dinner Shanti asked Kedarnath why he broke his promise to her and remarried. She also revealed intimate details about their relationship and their home that only Ludgi knew. Ludgi died a year before Shanti was born. Without a question of doubt Kedarnath knew this girl was Ludgi reincarnated.

Shanti's story spread through India and in 1935 came to the attention of Mahatma Gandhi, who appointed a panel of fifteen prominent people to accompany and observe the girl on a train trip to Mathura. Without a map she found her own way from the station to her previous home and, just like she had said, it was across the road from the Dwarkadhish temple.

Shanti Devi's life was well documented and investigated, and is still regarded as one of the best examples of children's past-life memories.

Perhaps you have noticed your child getting flashbacks like little Jeanette did when she was a baby. One day, while she was sitting on the kitchen floor watching her mother cooking, Jeanette piped up and said, 'I used to do that when you were a baby.' What was so startling about this comment was that Jeanette was too young to talk yet!

Children get flashbacks because they can easily access their visions from the places that they've lived in before because they are actually hardwired into their soul memory.

As a kid, I loved bonfire night, which we had once a year in the middle of June. A few nights before my eleventh birthday we lit the bonfire and oohed and aahed at the brilliant burst of colours splashing against the jet black sky. The bonfire burnt away into the small hours of the morning. When I got up the next day I walked through the shroud of smoke that lingered in the backyard. I still remember the surreal feeling of stepping back in time and seeing myself walking around the outskirts of a medieval castle. The battle was over, fires were burning in small piles over the bleak landscape. I knew this place well. It was my home. I walked into the castle and my children came up and gave me the biggest embrace and I could actually feel the love, as though I was being hugged right there in the present. Since that moment waves of memories have occasionally lapped at the shores of my mind, compelling me to explore that time in history. I developed a love of all things medieval—the history, clothes, architecture, books and art. Even now as I write I can see images of the Bayeux tapestry in my mind, the stone sculptures of women and knights in cathedrals from the Middle Ages.

Without being indoctrinated Tristan developed a strong love of all things medieval too. It's in his genes! By the age of three he was tearing up the hallway with shield and sword, fighting battles with imaginary knights, building Lego castles and watching *Ivanhoe* about a squillion times.

One night, when he was about nine, he yelled out in pain while sleeping. I rushed to his room and found him nursing his foot.

'What's wrong?' I asked.

His eyes were half shut. 'Take it out!' he cried.

'Take what out?' I said.

'The sword, that knight has wounded me with his sword. Take it out, it hurts so much.'

Then Tristan opened his eyes wide and looked around the bedroom. 'What happened to the battle?' he asked, bewildered.

'You were having a dream,' I told him.

He shook his head, 'No, it was too real. I was back in medieval times. My foot still hurts.'

I explained that he had a past-life dream, recalling a battle he actually experienced during a past life. The pain was real—his foot physically hurt—because he was reliving his personal history.

Are past lives and reincarnation real? More and more researchers, like Dr Brian Weiss who wrote the groundbreaking book *Many Lives, Many Masters*, believe so. In 1980, when Dr Weiss was the head of psychiatry at a university-affiliated hospital in Miami, he discovered the importance of past lives while conducting a hypnosis session with a troubled client named Catherine. He discovered that all of her fears, such as a fear of choking, water, aeroplanes and the dark, came from past lives. Under hypnosis Catherine revisited these past lives and managed to clear traumatic experiences that played out as fears in this lifetime and she made a remarkable recovery.

I should really mention that there are some wonderfully beautiful past-life memories and gifts that your child can bring forward. For example, if they were a healer in a previous life, they will be naturally gifted with either healing hands or a desire to help nurture other kids. It's like second nature to them. Or perhaps they have a flair for music because they were once a composer? In fact, quite a lot of your child's innate talents stem from experiences they had in past lives and they are now working positively with these talents.

How do you find out what lives they have had? You can ask them directly. Another method is to get them to tell you a story from another time and place—surprisingly, many kids create stories that are actually retrieved from their cellular memory banks unwittingly. Discovering your child's past lives can be a wonderful and fascinating journey for both of you.

12
THE TIME TUNNEL

Not only can they tap into past lives, psychic kids can also plug into the future. Clairvoyant kids can get regular visions of what is to come, while others get sporadic episodes, and some only do it once or twice during their childhood. Regardless, it is still an incredible ability to behold because they are moving past lineal time and space to reach into a dimension full of unfolding events that will play out as reality one day.

Being able to look through a time tunnel and see the future can be reassuring for them because they know what to expect and this helps them to plan around events. As you know, children thrive on routine as it gives them structure and with structure come security and comfort because they know what to expect. Well, the same applies with knowing future events. Your psychic child can use this knowledge to give themselves a structure to work around because they know how things might potentially pan out from their vision.

Of course, on the flip side it could be argued that there is always the possibility they might see or feel something unsettling. In situations like this, talking to them about what they have sensed or seen can help them put it into perspective and give them tools to deal with it so they don't feel overwhelmed. Unfortunately, like everything else in life, there is polarity—the positive and the challenging.

It is always wise to remember that, in general, psychic kids are usually shown what they need to see. I have been psychic all my life and I learnt very early on that if I am shown the future, I am not necessarily shown everything I want to know but what I need to know. My spirit guides will only give me what they feel is essential for me to know. They do not waste time trying to scare little kids because it is fun; besides, it is not in their nature to hurt. Spirit guides are benevolent divine beings so they always have our welfare at heart.

I know that certain kids do not always access their information from spirit guides; they might tap directly into the Akashic Records. The Akashic Records, or the Book of Life, is a realm in the spirit world that includes the collective consciousness and collective unconsciousness, and holds a record of every thought, feeling and action taken by people throughout history. It also holds the future. Even in these cases you can still counsel and guide your child to understand and deal with what they see.

For me, whether it was something fantastic that was going to happen at school or visions of what was going to happen on the global scene, my inner knowing knew that these glimpses of the future had a purpose. This is what people tend to overlook. You might get a vision, or an intuitive impression, that doesn't make sense right now, but one day it will.

Your child might see or feel something in their psychic time tunnel that comes true within hours, days or months, but occasionally the event won't happen for years. And, while they might not fully understand or appreciate what is happening, the day will come when the piece of the puzzle falls into place.

When your child tells you, 'Hey, I'm going to make a new friend tomorrow,' you might not think much about the comment. Then they add, 'It's a new kid that's going to join my class and they've got blond hair,' and it may grab a little more of your attention. But when they come home from school the following day and announce that they have a new blond-haired friend, you know that they were being psychic all along. Life is peppered with these kinds of experiences but it is not until something dramatic happens that we sit up and pay attention to their talents.

When she was eleven years old Fi and her family were on a bus tour holiday around the South Island of New Zealand. Part of the itinerary was a light-plane flight over breathtaking Milford Sound. Her parents were excited after managing to secure some of the limited seats on the flight but Fi was not. 'I'm not going with you, it's not safe!' she said bluntly.

Fi's parents tried to dismiss her fears by reminding her that she had never had a problem with light-plane flights before.

'They kept telling me that everything would be okay. But I didn't believe them,' Fi recalled. 'Nothing could change my mind because I had a strong feeling something was wrong. An image of a plane crashing jumped into my head. I knew I shouldn't leave the bus so I kept telling them, "The plane is not safe. I'm not getting on the plane!"'

When the bus arrived at the airstrip, the bus driver stood up and called out the names of the people on board who were going on the flight. On hearing her name called out aloud, Fi felt sick to the stomach.

'It felt terribly wrong, I could just feel it,' she told me. She turned to her parents and reiterated, 'It's not safe. I'm going to stay on the bus.' Fi was determined not to change her mind, much to her parents' disappointment. In the end they decided they wouldn't leave without her.

'The lovely Japanese couple who had been sitting behind us got our spot. They were really happy to get on the plane,' Fi said.

Three hours later Fi and her parents were sitting in their motel room watching the news on TV when the announcement came: 'Charter plane with engine trouble crashes over Milford Sound. There were no survivors.'

The family went into shock. They couldn't believe that the plane they were meant to be on had crashed.

'Pictures of the passengers from our tour bus appeared on the TV screen,' said Fi. 'I couldn't get the picture of the nice Japanese couple who had taken our place out of my mind. My mother started crying. She cried for the dead but she also cried tears of relief because we were safe.'

Was it a coincidence that Fi felt the plane was going to crash? Deep down inside she intuitively knew something terrible was going to happen. She had travelled on lots of charter flights before and the thought of flying had never bothered her until this fateful day when her intuitive ability guided her away from certain death.

You don't need a dramatic scenario to play out to appreciate the wonderful gifts your child has. Listen carefully and you can reap the rewards of their insights.

13

ANGEL BY MY BED

Fi was guided by her intuition. Sometimes kids' intuitive impressions come directly from the guidance of angels and spirit guides. They might not actually see them but they can often feel their presence.

Millions of kids believe in angels. It gives them a sense of faith, hope and, most importantly, security. The idea that they are being watched over by a lofty, powerful guardian angel has helped lots of kids get through the night. I met mine in the strangest way when I was twelve.

At the time my cousin Rose lived across the road. Every time I went to visit I loved looking at the awe-inspiring picture of a guardian angel that hung on the wall above her bed. There was something comforting in the angel's serenely beautiful face. She also had golden wings and halo and was wearing a flowing white garment with a hint of iridescent blue. The guardian angel seemed so fluid that she appeared to merge with the wash of water of the raging river beneath her. Against the dark of night, this angel was a blaze of light that illuminated the way for two barefoot children who were crossing a small dilapidated wooden footbridge by themselves. She was clearly protecting them and leading them to safety.

I wanted the same painting to hang over my own bed. I thought if I had a picture, then a real angel would stand by my bed and keep me safe, especially during sleepless nights.

One night, I sensed myself slipping out of my body. It scared the hell out of me. I thought I was dying. I didn't realise back then that it was only my astral body, part of the soul, which can leave the body and journey to the spirit world. Your astral body does this as a matter of course whenever you start dreaming. As no one had ever explained this to me, I was terrified that if I went back to sleep that night I would die.

In the muted darkness, my mahogany wardrobe looked strange. The natural grain of the timber on the left-hand panel looked like one of the scary trees from Disney's *Snow White*. The tree's face kept staring back at me from the wardrobe until I jumped out of bed and ran into the lounge room and turned on the TV. In between watching TV I tried closing my eyes, but I couldn't shake the memory of that slipping sensation of leaving my body or of the creepy wardrobe. I felt very alone and vulnerable, so I kept saying to myself, 'I wish I had my own angel. I wish my guardian angel was here right now.'

I repeated this prayer over and over but when nothing happened I finally decided to get up and change the channel. Several minutes later the TV screen went whitish and the sound stopped completely. I couldn't understand what was wrong with the television. Suddenly, the image of a luminous being appeared on the screen and it was staring directly at me! At first I thought, 'Oh my god, it's Jesus on the TV . . . I must be dying!' Whatever it was, it was definitely supernatural. The image of the luminous being got stronger, until it seemed to be projecting out from the TV. I don't know how long I was staring at the screen. It must have been more than five minutes. I was expecting the regular program to return but it didn't. It felt as though some strange force had taken over the TV and, in this protracted moment, time was being stretched. Then an eerie humming sound began reverberating around the room. I wanted to change the channel, but something inside me said, 'No, don't touch it. Leave it here.'

'Could this be my angel?' The thought was like a lightning bolt. Was I really lucky enough to get my own guardian angel? The lounge room was bathed in the white light emanating from the screen. I felt the strangest energy move through me. It filled me with calm and a sense of reassurance that it was okay to go back to bed. I now knew wasn't going to die.

Relieved, I returned to my bedroom and slid under the sheets. 'It's okay,' I reminded myself as I looked at the scary face on the wardrobe. 'Nothing bad is going to happen to me now.'

As I looked up at the ceiling I saw the image of my angel. I trusted that she was there. I had asked for one, and I believed she was with me. The energy in my bedroom shifted, it felt lighter and brighter. Then I felt a wisp of energy brush against my skin, like someone had run across it with a feather.

'Thank you, guardian angel,' I whispered and, closing my eyes, feel asleep.

Children often talk about seeing angels. They see them standing by their bedside, walking alongside them on their way home from school and even hovering over them ministering healing energies. If your child starts talking about seeing angels, why not ask them some questions about their ethereal visitors? Find out what kind of angels they are and why they are here. Perhaps you can tune in for yourself and feel their beautiful energy. It would be lovely to keep this link between heaven and earth open.

14

LITTLE
MESSENGERS

Another link between heaven and earth occurs when the
psychic child takes on the role of a go-between, becoming the
messenger connecting two worlds. They start seeing or hearing
people who have passed away or crossed over. These apparitions
can be frightening, as they come without warning. But most kids
who are lucky enough to experience one of these visitations are
usually touched by a feeling of happiness and love because they
are actually apparitions of deceased family members.

They come in from the spirit world to watch over you from
time to time, especially if you're going through a rough patch.
Your child, playing a go-between, can link you to them and pass
on messages that can make it seem much easier to find closure.
Imagine being given the reassurance that your loved one is now

safe and happy wherever they may be and your feelings of guilt or grief can be eased.

Spirits pass messages to your little go-between to let you know that everything happened just as it should and now you can get on with life because you know they are safe and well. Also, isn't it comforting to know that they are never really far away from you?

A week after Debbie's youngest brother Mark passed away, her seven-year-old daughter Leah came to her with a remarkable message. Mark was born with spina bifida and spent most of his twenty-one years confined to a wheelchair. Developmentally and physically delayed, and continually ill, he had a difficult life. Just before dawn, Leah went into Debbie's room and woke her up.

'Uncle Mark is here,' Leah exclaimed.

'What?' said Debbie.

'He's in the family room.'

Debbie's first reaction was that Leah had probably dreamt about him. But Leah was adamant that she saw him in person.

'Uncle Mark said, "Look, Leah, I'm standing. I can walk now and I am happy."'

Debbie sat up in bed. 'Did he tell you anything else?'

'Yes. He said, "I'm well. I don't feel sick anymore. I want you to tell Nan and Grandad that I am okay. I like it here."'

'Are you sure you didn't just dream about him?'

Leah shook her head and explained that he was a real person, as in flesh and blood. 'He was wearing a blue and white top with stripey thingies,' she said, 'and grey tracksuit pants.'

Debbie's parents were also surprised when she relayed the message. Of course, they questioned Leah, who told them the exact same story she had told Debbie. They were particularly astounded when she described Mark's clothes. These were actually the clothes

he was buried in, but Debbie's parents had not revealed this to anyone. They had chosen to dress him in the clothes that he always
loved and felt comfortable in—a blue and white checked flan-
nelette shirt and grey tracksuit pants. No one knew about this so
this detail convinced Leah's grandparents that she really had seen
Mark and was telling the truth.

Discovering that his spirit was free from pain and how happy he
was really made a difference to how they coped with his death. Hearing the words 'I don't feel sick anymore' was profoundly healing for
Mark's parents, who had watched him go through so much pain for
most of his life, and now they could let go of their concerns for him.
This simple but important message helped them to find closure.

To this day Leah is certain that she saw Uncle Mark that night.
She remembers the details with absolute clarity and her story has
never wavered.

'But it still made her feel very uneasy,' Debbie told me. 'There
have been many other incidents since then, and as she got older
she started experiencing bouts of insomnia.'

Leah became extremely anxious because she thought there was
something very wrong with her. Debbie tried to assure her that
everything was fine—Leah did well at school, had many friends
and was functioning normally as a young adult. But, when Leah
said she was hearing voices, Debbie became worried. 'Eventually,
when Leah was a teenager, she finally broke down and explained
that people were constantly bothering her by mumbling in her
ear at night.'

'Did the voices occur anywhere else other than in her bedroom?' I asked.

'No. She said it was only when she was lying quietly in bed at
night. Leah said it was as if people were talking around her.'

Debbie took Leah to see a doctor, not because she suspected anything was medically wrong, but because she needed to understand what was happening. Unfortunately, she didn't get any meaningful answers.

Soon afterwards Leah's psychic abilities grew stronger. She began seeing and hearing more spirits. She told her mother, 'I'm having weird things happen to me at night. People keep flashing pictures in my face.'

Leah also explained that there was one lady in particular who was bothering her. 'The pictures all look like something you would see on a replay of an old news reel on television,' she said. 'But there's one lady who keeps appearing in the news reel. I see her sitting on a park bench with a man dressed in an old army uniform.'

At the time neither Leah nor her mother could understand her psychic impressions, but months later when Debbie was looking through some of her grandfather's old family photos, Leah picked up a photo and was stunned.

'Who is this?' she asked. 'She's the one—the lady I told you about. Remember those old news reels in my head and that lady on the park bench?'

As it turns out the news flashes in her mind's eye were images of her great-grandmother who had married a soldier, Leah's great-grandfather, during World War I.

If your child ever sees an apparition, assure them most are quite harmless but they forget that we need our sleep! I gave Debbie some helpful tips on how Leah can stay psychically 'open' so she can work with her intuitive abilities while feeling confident in setting energetic boundaries. You can teach your child how to do this too.

One lovely but simple technique is to help them visualise a beautiful cocoon of golden light over their bed. Ask your child to call on their guardian angel and say, 'I would like not to be disturbed by spirits while I am sleeping. Tell them to talk to me only when I am awake.'

Being a go-between is a special psychic gift. But you need to make sure that your child isn't losing sleep by having too much spirit activity in the middle of the night. By teaching them to set up healthy energetic boundaries, you can help them create a win/win situation.

15
LINGERING VIBES

Your home is a lot busier than you think. Leah discovered that unexpected visitors do drop in from time to time. What confuses most parents is that their child is seeing something they cannot see or feel themselves. Have you ever felt that way? That you have been left out of the picture? The truth is that you are probably reacting to the energy unconsciously, only your conscious mind does not register the energies of spirit because they are very subtle.

Not only can children pick up vibes of your loved ones in spirit, they are pretty good at sensing other vibes too. Lingering vibes in the atmosphere are created by spirit visitors that are unknown or by people living in the house. Perhaps you have just received great news and your child runs into the room and is immediately infected with a sense of happiness from the exuberance in the air? Or when there has been an argument and the atmosphere is heavy? Children just know when something is out of kilter, just like Linda.

'When I was ten I was living at my great-grandfather's place in the north of Spain and my mother and her friend were playing with the ouija board daily,' Linda told me.

At the time Linda didn't understand what a ouija board, or séance, was. No one bothered to explain to her what they were doing. This went on for weeks until one day something strange started happening. Linda felt an uncomfortable vibe in the house, the atmosphere felt heavy.

'It was late at night and I got up to get a drink of water,' she said. 'I was alone in the kitchen and suddenly one of the glasses on the benchtop exploded! After that, one glass was exploding every single night. It always happened after midnight and everyone was asleep and we'd all wake up to this terrible noise.'

Linda's mother told her not to worry and it was probably just the result of washing the glasses with hot water. Linda was young but she wasn't stupid. Intuitively she knew that this wasn't the real reason, and she observed that when the glasses were washed with lukewarm water, it was still happening. 'The other odd thing,' she added, 'was that it was always only one glass per night that exploded.'

Linda was terrified, having no understanding of what was going on or why. Something paranormal was happening in the house.

Although Linda's experience was a little hair-raising, there are so many beautiful stories of kids who find comfort in feeling the vibes of family members in spirit. In my book *Sixth Sense* I mentioned how my teacher Rhondda's little daughter Catherine was always visited by her grandfather whenever she was sick. The only sound they ever heard wafting out of her room during the visits from her grandfather were soft coos and giggles.

Children can pick up on the presence of paranormal activity and it's no surprise that strange things were happening at Linda's great-grandfather's place because her mother was tampering with the ouija board. In her ignorance, her mother was summoning the spirits but she had no idea that one was going to hang around and leave a nightly calling card! The earthbound spirit in their house had a heavy energy, reflecting its inner melancholy. Just as we leave our vibes in our house—our happy vibes make our home warm and welcoming, and negative vibes make it unwelcoming—spirits can change the feel of the atmosphere in a place.

Unfortunately, lots of teenagers mess about with ouija boards and draw in the wrong energies. If you know of anyone playing with one, advise them about the dangers or at least teach them how to seal and protect their home with gold light, call on angels to protect the place and ask that only evolved souls be permitted to enter the session.

If your child is picking up on negative vibes, you can teach them how to change the atmosphere by simply visualising a beautiful, bright, happy and uplifting yellow light washing through the room and consuming all the negative vibes. Your child will love this exercise and it will empower them as well. Knowing that they can shift energies in the room means that they won't have to feel uncomfortable in their own home.

My daughter Chiara asked to have her bedroom painted yellow when she was five. The colour was so bright that for the first week I wore sunglasses every time I went in there. She laughed at me. But, do you know, she made the right intuitive choice—she always woke up happy and sang while she played with her toys in the yellow room. Colours have a psychological effect on us. Colours such as yellow are used to create happiness, blue to instil calmness, red to fire us up. Visitors immediately felt the lively, wonderful and joyful vibe of Chiara's room.

Places, like people, have an atmosphere. What atmosphere do you want to create in your home?

16

THE GIFT OF GIVING

Kids are wonderful. They use their inbuilt radar, or intuitive knowing, all the time, often without realising it. They trust their gut feeling. There's no long-winded debate about what they should or shouldn't do.

Intuition is also a sort of inner soul awakening. It is driven by an inner desire to do something or to pursue an interest that your soul has come here to experience. It's a feeling response to your soul urge which is directing you to start expressing skills and talents that you will master later on in life. A soul awakening isn't always obvious at the time, but when a child follows their intuition it can be incredibly powerful. Sometimes, when a child acts on this urge, they end up helping others too.

At nine I was a bit of a tomboy. I loved swinging off trees and running wild through paddocks. But, since I never seemed to get any dolls, I decided I wanted one. Every year there was a Christmas picnic held by Dad's employers. There were merry-go-rounds, fairy floss, three-legged races and pony rides. The crowning moment of the day was when Santa arrived on the back of a truck to hand out presents. We lined up in rows according to our ages, eagerly awaiting our gifts. Usually it was the same gift for each age every year and, since my sister Lena got a lovely delicately featured doll when she was nine, I couldn't wait to get mine.

That year my Christmas present was a dark ragdoll with woolly black hair. After the initial disappointment passed I started bonding with my doll. I called her Holly and kept her in a secret place under the house, next to Lena's beautiful doll. To me, Holly was the best thing ever.

One day after school we went under the house and discovered that my precious Holly was missing. I started searching frantically and a few minutes later I saw a black dog in the back of the yard near the tall tomato plants. He had something in his mouth. I raced towards him, but was too late. Pieces of Holly were scattered all over the yard.

I never realised how deeply this affected me. Over the years Holly became a distant memory that surfaced occasionally. One day my daughter Chiara and I were talking about toys and she asked me, 'What was your favourite dolly?'

'My ragdoll Holly, but I didn't get to keep her for long.'

'Why not?' she asked.

I explained what had happened to Holly and nothing more was mentioned.

Six months later Chiara spent the morning helping my cousin Rose with some chores. Rose gave her pocket money and then they went down to the local fair. Chiara came home with a small present for me. I was surprised as Chiara usually spent her pocket money on herself or her friends.

'I know you're going to love it,' she beamed. 'I just felt you needed to have it. Hurry up and open it!'

When I unwrapped the package I was deeply moved to find a small dark ragdoll with a red checked dress.

'It's for you, Mummy. You need a dolly because you lost yours. I've called her Holly the Dolly.'

Chiara took Holly out of my hands and placed her on my dressing table, facing the bed. 'Now you can look at her every day,' she commented.

I looked at Holly and a strange sensation washed through me. Then it hit home. I got a clear vision in my third eye of the link between losing my special doll and a strong behavioural pattern I had been playing out for years.

Why didn't I realise it sooner? Isn't it funny how your subconscious mind still stores the everyday traumas that your conscious mind likes to bury?

I had always found it hard accepting gifts from other people, especially people I had helped. I would say, 'No thanks,' or 'Really, I didn't do anything to deserve it.' And I also kept giving away things that I bought for myself. It got to the point where I would sabotage buying things for myself, often saying 'I'll get it next week,' and then end up spending the money on the kids or someone else.

I finally joined the dots. The reason I pushed gifts away was because deep down inside, I was expecting these things I love to be taken from me. That subconscious pattern began on the day Holly was destroyed by the neighbours' dog. Part of me didn't want to relive my childhood trauma of losing the thing I loved the most, so I had detached myself from owning special things.

Another interesting parallel was that Chiara was nine when she gave me the new doll and I was nine when I lost Holly. The circle was complete.

Chiara is a natural-born healer and counsellor, and a part of her soul purpose was slowly awakening—the desire to help and heal others. She was guided by her intuition, which told her that this present would have a special significance. It was more than just replacing the old doll. Her soul knew that it was going to heal part of my own inner child. And it did. After that I found it so much easier to accept gifts and to buy myself special things.

Stay open to the small gestures and gifts your children give you. They often know what you need, even if you don't. And their gifts, like Holly, can actually trigger a healing deep within you.

17
SEEING COLOURS AROUND PEOPLE

I have always been open to the strong psychic impressions my kids get because I feel there is something intrinsically beautiful about the way children intuitively see the world with their sixth sense. This is especially so when they are able to see colours around people.

When they see rainbows around someone, what they are actually seeing are the colours of the person's soul. Some children can feel a person's soul essence. Others just know what is happening emotionally, psychologically and physically by the colours in their aura. It is their wonderful insight into human nature that makes many psychic children a lot more tolerant and sympathetic. It is a great pity that so many kids end up blocking this ability.

When Tristan was six years old he came home from school one

day and said, 'Sue [he never calls me 'Mum'], you won't believe it, but Ally's face was all green today!'

'Green?' I said.

'Yes,' he replied enthusiastically. 'We were drawing and every time I looked up I kept seeing a green light around her face and shoulders.'

'That's nice,' I said. 'Do you see colours around other kids?'

'Yes, all the time. I see rainbow colours in bits and pieces around them,' he explained.

'Why haven't you told me about this before?' I asked. I allowed my kids to unfold their abilities naturally. I waited until they approached me with a question and then I would explain the phenomena they were experiencing. It is wise to never push psychic kids; encourage, yes, but don't stress them out by pushing them too far too quickly.

Tristan shrugged his shoulders. 'I thought everyone sees them.'

'Have any other kids talked to you about it?'

'No,' he said. 'But I thought it was because we all see them, so there's nothing to talk about.'

I learnt a valuable lesson that day. Just because children don't talk about their psychic experiences doesn't mean they aren't having them. Kids often keep things to themselves. And, like Tristan, many kids feel that everyone is in the same boat, so there's no need for comment.

If your child starts talking about seeing colours around people, why not ask them things like, 'What colours do you see around me?' or 'What do you feel these colours mean?' Get them to delve into the colours because the colours in your aura reflect your emotional, psychological and even physical wellbeing. For example, if they see pink in your aura, it means you are giving out lots of unconditional love. However, if there is a murky pink, you need a lot of TLC. Also, this sort of encouragement will assure them that their psychic vision is perfectly natural and worth exploring. I have included a Colour Ready Reckoner chart at the back of this book to help you and your child understand the spiritual meaning behind each colour.

Another great tip is to suggest to your child that they occasionally keep an eye on changes they see in auras. They can monitor these changes by doing a simple drawing of the aura they see around you or one of their friends. Once they have finished that task ask them to write down what they feel these colours represent. Then wait a few weeks and ask them to look at the same auras again.

Have the colours remained unchanged? If they haven't changed then the person is pretty much in the same space they were in a few weeks ago. However, if the colours have changed, for example, your child drew a lot of yellow in the first picture and it changed to blue in the second drawing, then something has shifted within that person. Ask your child to tell you why they think the colours have changed.

Colours in our aura change regularly in response to how we think and feel and the kind of experiences we are having. For example, if the aura is yellow it can mean that you are spending a lot of time in your head thinking about things, or you are feeling very empowered. When your aura changes to blue it can indicate that you are now focused on communication issues like needing to speak your truth.

By monitoring changes in the auras they see your child will strengthen their sixth sense as well as developing a great feel for where people are at.

18
STAYING OPEN

It was perfectly natural for Tristan to see auras because his psychic channel was always open. He didn't struggle with it, it just seemed to flow. Children like Tristan find making the transition from psychic kid to psychic adult easier because there are no obstacles holding back their ability. But it's not this way for everyone.

One question parents ask me is, 'Why do some kids stay psychically open while others block or lose this ability?'

I feel it's a very important question because if you understand what factors hinder a child's psychic development then you can take positive action to remedy the situation.

There are reasons why this happens. Sometimes it's because their talent wasn't supported by their immediate environment. But there is also another reason why a child closes down.

There's a turning point in a child's life at age seven when destiny puts a fork in the road. At seven, they choose the road of critical thinking or the road of intuitive thinking. Those who choose critical thinking start to override their psychic ability, until it shuts down. Either way I find the decision made is always the right one at the time. Their choice is often affected by their karma, what they need as a soul to know and grow. Karma is the universal law of cause and effect that shapes the ebb and flow of life experiences that come your way.

Before your child incarnates they choose who they want for parents, the gifts they wish to develop and the life journey they want to experience. It might be in your child's karma to stay psychically open. But, then again, they may have to go through a period when they shut off their sixth sense or find it difficult to work with. However, it is reassuring to know that at some stage down the road they can reawaken this wonderful ability. In the meantime, if your child has stopped using their psychic ability, don't be alarmed. It is not uncommon for this to happen when the age of reason kicks in. This is the time when children experience a new level of awareness, moving past what is called base-chakra consciousness.

Your child experiences base-chakra consciousness from birth until age seven. This is when they are developing their life foundations, taking on beliefs and attitudes that will follow them into adulthood. During the first three years especially, they learn about being physical, the importance of having shelter and feeling secure. They try to find their place in the 'tribe' and develop their sense of individuality. Then at seven, just before they move forward to the next stage in their spiritual development, they have a spiritual crisis.

As they stand on the threshold of sacral-chakra consciousness— the chakra which helps them explore their emotional landscape and how to deal with relationships—many kids go through a particularly sensitive rite of passage: they develop a fear of death which can last days, weeks or even months. Children don't know why they suddenly become anxious about death. One minute they are blissfully unaware of it, and then there's a change. I know both my kids experienced this. I particularly remember Chiara running out of the classroom every morning for nearly six weeks.

'Don't go, Mummy!' she pleaded.

'Why?' I asked.

She started crying. She couldn't tell me what was scaring her.

One day the teacher followed her out. 'Don't worry,' she said to me. 'A lot of kids go through this. She's at an age when she's starting to think about death. It's a phase kids go through.'

When I looked back, I remembered that my son Tristan did the same thing when he was seven.

Having the fear of death surfacing at seven is a perfectly natural emotional and psychological response. It is a stepping-stone away from early childhood, and the idea that the world revolves around them, into an awareness that it doesn't. At this point they allow their thoughts to override their gut instinct. Some cultures encourage children to work equally with the left (logical) and right (creative/intuitive) sides of the brain, allowing children to continue to access their intuition. The foundation years between birth and seven are a critical phase in a child's development. If you pay attention to what your child is saying about the strange things they're seeing or experiencing, talk with them about it and help them make sense of it, then their sixth sense doesn't have to shut down in favour of critical thinking by the time they reach seven.

You can support them during this phase by giving them Bach flower or Australian bush flower remedies, which both work on treating emotional and psychological issues to help them shift underlying fears. Another tip is to teach them to focus on deep breathing while they are feeling stressed, or even repeating an affirmation like, 'I am feeling secure in my world', which can help them regain a sense of personal control and empowerment through this period of change.

Kids can use drawings and meditation techniques to keep the intuitive side of the brain open. Ask your child to do a drawing of their hand. Get them to use their less dominant hand to draw with while they observe the detail of the shape and lines in the other hand. The key to this exercise is to make sure that they fight the urge to look down at the paper to see if what they are drawing is right. This technique is designed to frustrate the left side of the brain which wants to maintain control by checking to see if the drawing is perfect. I know a lot of artists who use this exercise whenever they are feeling intuitively blocked.

If your child prefers meditation then get them to close their eyes and visualise themselves in a beautiful place. Suggest to them that they can meet their spirit guide who will show them a glimpse of the future.

Your child can enjoy the benefits of having the logical mind kick in without sacrificing the wonderful gifts that come with working with the creative and intuitive mind.

19
TALKING TO ANIMALS

As well as their amazing ability to see people's auras, kids also have a fantastic knack for tuning into animals. They intuitively know what their pets are trying to say, what they need. Over the years I have watched Tristan and Chiara share a wonderful psychic bond with our dog Bodo, or, as we think of him, their brother. How about you? When you were young, did you have a special connection with one of your pets or a type of animal? Does your child?

Animals, like humans, are very psychic, so we have this marvellous psychic connection going on where language isn't needed. My kids sense when Bodo is happy and sad, when he wants to go for a walk, when he needs a hug, when he is hungry and when something is unsettling him — without relying on the usual physical cues. Sure, we can look at him wagging his tail when he is happy, or licking his lips when he wants a drink of water, but it goes deeper than that. Bodo also knows what we need and gives unconditionally. Remarkably, he does not even bark when he calls me, he makes a doggy kind of 'maaa' sound, especially when he really wants me to listen to him or when he protests about something.

While it's lovely to observe your child sensing what your own pet needs, it is eye-opening when they psychically pick up on the needs of animals they don't know.

Our 'visitor' entered the front yard unannounced but by the time he walked onto the front veranda Bodo was racing down the hall, doing his 'Look at me, aren't I a good boy, I'm protecting the home' thing and barking like mad. Both Tristan and Chiara ran to the front door to see what the all the commotion was about.

'There's a black dog on the doorstep,' yelled Tristan, remaining behind the security screen.

The black doberman did not leave when I arrived.

'Look at his back,' said Chiara.

He had a terrible skin condition. We couldn't see a collar on him.

'He's sad. He needs food and water,' said Tristan. 'He's been lost for days.'

'How do you know that he has been lost for days?' I asked. 'He may have just left his home an hour ago.'

'No, he's been lost for lots of days,' Tristan replied.

'I'll get a blanket for him to sit on,' offered Chiara.

'Hang on, guys, you don't know anything about this dog. He could bite you,' I warned.

'No,' said Chiara. 'No, he won't bite. He just wants somewhere to stay.'

My intuition matched my children's so we led him through the side gate into the courtyard and I watched my kids tend to him.

A neighbour came over and said, 'Are you mad? Now the dog will never go.'

Tristan told her, 'He'll go when he's ready. He's staying here because he needs rest to get better.'

'Yes,' said Chiara, throwing her five cents in. 'He wants to go back to his family.'

My neighbour looked at me. 'Are you sure? He might have been dumped. There's no dog tag on his collar.'

As it turned out, he may have been a large dog with big teeth but he was the perfect guest. We left the side gate open for him to go if he wanted but he did not go far. He walked from the courtyard to the front yard then back again. He seemed content to stay at our place and have the kids attend to his every need! And they loved looking after him because they knew he needed care. He was a blessing because he brought out the nurturing side of my kids and they learnt a lot about what animals need from this unexpected visitor.

Three days later when we arrived home from school the dog was no longer there.

'He's not coming back,' said Chiara. 'He's gone home.'

Children who don't have pets can still psychically bond with animals. Perhaps you have noticed that your child has been drawn to connect to an animal at a particular time? Listen to what they have to say about these animals. For example, your child might be drawn to a lamb at an animal farm. Ask them, 'Why did you prefer spending time with the lamb instead of the ducklings, calf or piglet?' Intuitively, they might be drawn to a specific animal because it needs their attention, or it might have qualities that your kid relates to.

Occasionally your child might talk about their 'imaginary' pet. Sometimes they are playing make believe; other times they are actually seeing the spirit of an animal and talking to them the same way you might talk to your deceased grandfather.

Whether it is your own pet or a stray, kids can sense dangerous animals from loving ones, the sick from the healthy, and the needy from the mischievous. They are psychic enough to be animal whisperers.

20

IN THE TWILIGHT ZONE

Blessings don't always come wrapped up in neat little boxes. Sometimes, they happen in surreal circumstances. So even if your child has never shown pronounced psychic abilities, they can end up surprising you by doing something extraordinary, like saving your life.

At eleven, Alicia knew the rules. Her parents' room was strictly out of bounds. But one night something happened to make her break the rules.

'I don't know how to explain it,' Alicia told me. 'I got up at night and something came over me, so I was like me but I wasn't me. I didn't feel right. My body was moving but I didn't feel like it was my body. I couldn't tell it what to do. It was doing it all on its own. I remember going up to my parents' bedroom. I couldn't stop myself, even though I knew I would get in a lot of trouble.'

'So you had no control whatsoever?' I asked.

'None. It was weird,' she said. 'As I was walking up the stairs, a voice in the back of my head reminded me that I would get in trouble from my parents. I knew this but at the same time the feeling that came over me, this force that was guiding me, was stronger.'

'Did you try to fight it?'

'No, by the time I was outside my parents' bedroom I went with the flow. I didn't understand what was happening but I knew that I had to let my body do what it was doing.'

'You were having a twilight zone moment?' I said with a smile, referring to the sensation we occasionally feel during a paranormal experience. You sense that whatever is going on is happening outside of your normal daily reality. It also refers to moments when your subconscious mind takes over your actions.

'Do you think it was your subconscious mind?' I asked.

'I honestly don't know. It could have been. Maybe it was an angel or my spirit guide, I really don't know. I remember opening the bedroom door and I walked over to my father's side of the bed. My hands reached out and lifted the heavy winter bedcovers off him and I started shouting, "Dad! Mum!"

'Suddenly I saw a fire coming up from the mattress. My father sat up screaming, his arms were burning. Both my parents jumped out of the bed. They were in shock. Initially, neither of them knew what was going on. Then my mum ran and got water to put out the fire while Dad tried to beat the flames down with a pillow.

'I just stood there waiting for them to yell at me for being in their room. But they didn't.'

Alicia later found out that her father had been very drunk when he went to bed. He decided to have a cigarette and fell asleep while it was still alight. The cigarette burnt through the mattress which started smouldering. When Alicia lifted the bedcovers a rush of oxygen fuelled the fire. Within seconds it created huge flames.

'Did you ever work out what led you to your parents' room?' I asked her.

She shook her head. 'It was years ago. I don't know if I was in some kind of trance. I had no control but I know it must have been something good that entered my body, or intuitively guided me, because I ended up saving my parents' lives.'

Life doesn't always give us neat or definitive answers as to why things come to pass the way they do. Strange things do happen. The ordered world we live in is often peppered with a twist of the bizarre or a splash of the unbelievable to remind us there is a lot more to reality than we're told about. It's during these moments when some kind of intervention stops accidents, averts tragedies or produces miracles that we realise there is a greater force working in the backdrop of our lives. We can't always explain why a paranormal event takes place. The important thing is to recognise that they are real. Even if such an event only occurs once, in that precious moment when your child has tapped into an unknown source, or into their own psychic ability, you get a blessing you will cherish for life.

21
AMAZING LITTLE ARTISTS

Another unknown source your child may be capable of tapping into is psychic artwork. It's a beautiful way of capturing what they sense or see, and it helps them share their vision with you. Often parents complain of how frustrating it is not being able to see what their children see. You can share part of their psychic journey by getting your child to draw. As I mentioned earlier, drawing can be a valuable tool and can help children to provide evidence that what they are sensing is very real. But you can take it one step further, by encouraging them to explore their inner and outer world through art. Kids feel comfortable expressing themselves through their drawing; they don't get caught up in trying to find the right words, or feel that you're not on the same page with them. Pictures are a great way of getting a two-way flow of communication going as well.

As a child living on her parents' country property 'Bella Vista', Elizabeth used to see what she called 'ghosts'. Not surprisingly, her younger brother Greg did too.

When she was on her own Elizabeth used to see a tall skinny man wearing a top hat while Greg, when alone, would see a shorter plump guy wearing a bowler hat. It was only when they were together that they would both see the two ghosts walking down towards the shearing shed and occasionally out the back near the well.

Greg's ghost became adventurous, becoming a frequent bedside visitor and prompting Greg to complain, 'The short fat guy is sitting on my bed. He's bouncing on it.'

One night, a friend slept over and, of course, he knew nothing about Greg's ghostly visitor. In the middle of the night the friend woke up and called out, 'Greg, who's that man with the funny hat that's bouncing on the end of the bed?'

Meanwhile Elizabeth was having her own night-time drama. The tall skinny guy with the top hat loved hanging around near the bathroom. Too frightened to go to the bathroom alone, she would yell out to her mother, 'I need to go to the toilet, Mummy. Come now!' No matter how desperate she was to go to the toilet, Elizabeth would wait until her mother woke up and came to hold her hand and walk with her to the bathroom.

Every so often Elizabeth would tell her mother that she also saw her grandfather, who they called Poppa Tom, in the bathtub and that he seemed to be laughing at her. On one occasion she exclaimed, 'Poppa Tom is sitting in a funny position, he's not moving.'

To help relieve her fears, her mother got Elizabeth to draw the visions of Poppa Tom and the two ghosts hanging around on the farm. The next day, the phone rang. Elizabeth picked it up and instinctively said to the lady on the other end of the phone, 'Poppa Tom is dead.' It was an immediate, intuitive reaction and she didn't realise that the lady was a nurse at the hospital. Her mother walked into the room just as Elizabeth was relaying this message. 'Poppa Tom is dead,' she repeated, looking her mother straight in the eye as she hung up the phone.

A few minutes later the phone rang again. Elizabeth promptly answered, saying, 'I've already told Mummy that Poppa has died.' Her mother grabbed the phone and spoke with the nurse who informed her that Poppa Tom had been rushed to the hospital after being found unconscious in his bath but unfortunately it was too late.

A few years later Elizabeth's family sold the farm and the new owners did some research on the history of Bella Vista, which they had renamed 'Keston'.

'They showed my father photos of the previous owners,' Elizabeth told me. 'We were shocked to discover that the two men Greg and I used to see were actually previous owners of the farm. The weird thing is that the tall skinny man with the top hat and the short fat man with the bowler hat had owned the farm at different times. And, both the men in the photos were the splitting image of the pictures I had drawn of them.'

Elizabeth was doing what is known as psychic art. There are some wonderfully talented kids out there who capture the very essence of souls in spirit in their drawings. It's definitely something not to be overlooked—it's amazing how accurate they can be, as Elizabeth was. Perhaps you have seen a psychic artist performing at an event like a Mind Body Spirit festival? Some psychic artists specialise in drawing spirits who are watching over you, such as your spirit guide.

While sceptics might claim that these drawings are nothing more than the product of an overactive imagination, and I can understand why they think that, it does not mean they are. This is why it's so important that a psychic artist passes on a valid piece of information to accompany the drawing and substantiate their vision. When I first visited a psychic artist, she drew my spirit guide and he looked exactly as I intuitively saw him — an ancient Egyptian man bathed in iridescent indigo and blues. She also passed on a message for my mother which we later validated. She was right on the ball. This was no coincidence.

Drawing is such a beautiful medium to work with. It's intuitive, fluid and captures the visions we see. Kids who draw their visions are psychic artists and there's no limit to their talent. Whether it's a loved one in spirit, a spirit guide, guardian angel or even a dimensional realm within a different world that your child is drawing, it would be fantastic if this kind of ability could flourish.

22
PSYCHIC KIDS' NETWORK

If kids are sensitive enough to see and draw apparitions, it makes you wonder what else they can do. As a psychic, I know that they can sense so much more than they tell you about. Although kids have their own unique way of working with their psychic senses, they do not necessarily always share what they see and feel with parents. Sometimes, kids have a secret language of their own, one that other kids intuitively pick up and share with each other, while leaving grown-ups in the dark. I call it the psychic kids' bush telegraph.

Several years ago, my ex-husband Stephen and I were called into the oncology ward at a large children's hospital. Tasha, a student of ours, was a nurse who worked in that ward. Strange things were happening there and she wasn't the only one who noticed them—the doctors did too. One day the doctors had had enough and asked Tasha to call us to take care of the paranormal activity.

If you have ever been inside a children's oncology ward, you would have probably felt waves of conflicting thoughts and emotions. It's confronting to see so many terminally ill children. But did you know that some of these thoughts and feelings you are experiencing aren't always your own? You are actually reacting to the residual energy hanging around a place.

Residual energy is a film of 'dumped' energy. By this I mean pockets of energy created by your thoughts and feelings. You see, every thought and feeling you have is an expression of energy. Your energy creates a vibe, an essence that others pick up around you and even in your home, where your vibes linger in the atmosphere. For example, if there's lots of laughter and happiness around you, then that vibe resonates in the air. Visitors immediately react to this residual energy, feeling relaxed and comfortable because your home has the feel-good factor. But when you walk into a place where people have been constantly bickering, you will feel edgy and uncomfortable yourself. Your sixth sense helps you pick up and react to these vibes.

You cannot miss the mix of raw emotion and unsteady thoughts, hope and despair lingering in the air in a cancer ward. Usually, it's been created by parents and other family members visiting the sick child. They've got no idea that they are dumping their emotional and psychological baggage there, but that's exactly what they are doing. It's a natural thing to do. And patients can also pick up on it and it can often make them feel uncomfortable. But there's another thing going on. These special kids psychically send messages to each other. They sense the vibes and they know what's going on around them, even though it is unspoken.

When we were there, Tasha was telling us how the kids who were in remission on one side of the ward often knew what was happening in the other part of the ward where the children were terminally ill. No one told them—the staff didn't talk about it, nor did the parents, but the kids intuitively knew. The kids' psychic network was alive and well. They often knew when one of their friends was going to pass away before they were actually told. Some kids could even see spirits hanging around their dying friend. These spirits are family members and spirit guides assigned to support the dying child, to soothe them and to escort them into the spirit world. How comforting for parents and loved ones to discover that a child didn't die alone.

We were taken to two rooms used by terminally ill children. Standing outside the first I felt sick to the stomach and sad. I got an image of a young boy who was screaming in pain yet he kept holding on. I learnt that he was seven years old and had a brain tumour. He knew he was dying, even though no one had told him, and he was okay with it. He was ready to die. But because his mother could not let him go, he kept fighting to stay alive despite the incredible pain. Walking into that room was heart-wrenching.

Then we went into the other room. It had an entirely different energy, it felt almost peaceful. But this was where a lot of the paranormal activity was happening, in this part of the ward and, in particular, this room.

We got the impression that a young Indigenous girl had just passed here. She was not the problem. I tuned in and felt the presence of her grandmother's spirit. She could not find her little girl so she was running amok through the ward, slamming doors shut, throwing objects around and leaving the atmosphere of her grief everywhere—everywhere but inside the room where her granddaughter died. We did a psychic rescue on the grandmother's soul, who was an earthbound lost soul, and opened a doorway to the spirit world and summoned her granddaughter. They were reunited and the paranormal activity stopped immediately. We also removed the heavy residual energy in these two rooms and replaced it with the energy of love and joy, to make these rooms as comfortable as possible for the kids who stay there before they cross over to the light.

Children's inner knowing always tells them the truth and this is no more apparent than in an oncology ward. Terminally ill kids often have an incredible level of acceptance and maturity beyond their age. You can see it in their eyes; they're saying, 'I know and it's okay.' This is the thing that really amazes me about kids—how some of them accept death and know that it is okay to cross over. Despite being so young, they are able to see the reality and, in many instances, especially when they are loved and cared for, they are not afraid to die. There is less fear of death and less likelihood of them becoming stuck between worlds when they are surrounded by people they love and by spirit guides. It's so much easier for them to trust in the great unknown.

23

IN SAFE HANDS

A lot of the psychic activity children encounter involves spirits and there is a reason for this. It's because spirits are a part of our lives. Spirit guides stand by us from the moment we draw the breath of life until we take our last. And, as I mentioned earlier, loved ones in spirit are regular visitors. One week it could be your grandfather, the next week a distant cousin could be hanging around. While you have a few permanent spirit guides by your side, others come and go as required. As for family, well, it's a policy of *mi casa es su casa*, or 'my house is your house', so you're never really alone!

Isn't it soothing and reassuring to know that even in your darkest moment Spirit is standing by shining a light for you? If you are *open* you will feel their comforting and supporting presence, and their messages and helpful advice can come through your third-eye chakra. But, if you stay *closed* and ignore your sixth sense impressions, this information won't flow through to your conscious mind. You are shutting off a vital psychic link between the two of you. Occasionally, answers do manage to slip through. Without realising it, you've received a message from Spirit but your logical mind might undermine it by telling you, 'My head found the solution'. But did it really?

Whether you're dealing with a major issue or trying to find direction, the true source of the visions that pop into your head, or solutions that come out of the blue, can actually be the voice of Spirit or your higher self, which is the highest aspect of your soul. The higher self is that part of you that knows the bigger picture. So, flanked by Spirit and your own inner guide, you are in good hands and the same goes for your psychic kid. And you are also in the custody of loved ones in spirit who take special care of you. It doesn't matter if you are celebrating a birthday, graduating or starting a new job, they're sharing your joy. Or, if you are feeling down, lost or distressed, they will stand by your side because of the strong bond of love. They are with you when you are born, and they will escort you when you pass over.

Did you realise that your spirit guides know what is going to happen before you do? They see the bigger picture, connecting the fragments of events in your life together. They know how the sequence of your life is going to play out and, yes, this means they factor in karma and your free will. It is one thing knowing that they know, but it's a different ball game when you are in the dark. What if you miss the signs and something happened that you feel could have been avoided? I've met people who have grieved what they perceived as being a mistake on their behalf because they should have paid more attention; they should not have missed the clues. Self-judgement does not help you get closure. Understanding why things turned out the way they did does. Your spirit helpers give you the answers you need at the time, and sometimes this entails getting only bits and pieces of the puzzle and not the whole story. Why? Perhaps you weren't meant to see it all, that certain events needed to happen exactly the way they did.

Four-year-old Jessica was a beautiful happy child. One day, while playing upstairs in her bedroom, a lovely lady appeared. She sat down on the floor and played 'tea' with Jessica and her dolls.

'Yes, thanks, I'd like a drink,' she said in a gentle voice. Jessica didn't question who this stranger was. She seemed nice so Jessica played with her and poured fruit juice from her toy porcelain teapot into the tiny cup and set it down next to her visitor.

'Thank you, Jessica,' she said.

'What's your name?' asked Jessica, looking at the dark-eyed woman with the long brown hair.

'It's Claire,' she responded. 'I'm going to be spending a lot of time with you.' And she did. Every day for nearly a week Claire popped into Jessica's bedroom and talked and played with her.

On the Saturday afternoon Jessica emerged from her bedroom and raced down the stairs and into the kitchen where her mother, Robbie, was preparing dinner.

'Mummy,' she began, as she sat up on the breakfast bar stool, 'the lovely lady said she is coming to take me away with her.'

'What lovely lady?' Robbie asked.

'The one with the long hair,' she replied. 'The one I play with.'

Her mother thought Jessica was playing with an imaginary friend and wasn't going to read anything more into it, until Jessica surprised her with an incredible piece of information.

'You know the lady, Mummy. You know her. Come, I'll show you.' Jessica took her mother into the hall and stopped in front of the Balinese carved timber stand with a row of picture frames on it. 'Her . . . this one,' she said, pointing to a picture of a young brunette with dark eyes.

'No, you've made a mistake, darling,' Robbie said. 'That's your Aunty Claire. You can't be playing with her. Aunty Claire is dead.' Claire had died in a car accident two years earlier. Robbie never really spoke to Jessica about her because she was still grieving the loss of her sister. Robbie thought Jessica was just used to seeing this photo and created her as the imaginary friend.

'She plays with me and my dollies,' Jessica was adamant. 'She said, "Everything is going to be okay, that she's going to take care of me from now on."'

The next morning, while they were playing at the park, Robbie got a flash of the image of a blue car speeding down the street. She tried dismissing the vision but it kept coming back. It didn't mean anything to her. What was a blue car supposed to mean?

They went home and Robbie started preparing lunch. Jessica said she was going to play outside. Less than twenty minutes later Robbie heard a loud, screeching car. She ran to the dining room window and looked outside. She saw a blue car speeding off down the street, just like in her vision. Then she saw Jessica crumpled down by the kerb.

'Why didn't I get it?' Robbie asked me. 'Why didn't I interpret the signs? She told me that Claire was coming to get her. I saw the blue car. Why couldn't I put the two together?' She was still angry, even though this event happened five years earlier. I can understand why she was feeling like this: how can anything ever replace the loss of a child? 'What happened to her soul? Where is she?'

I explained to her that Jessica crossed over peacefully and that 'upstairs' (as I call the spirit world) knew that the accident was going to happen. They were preparing her by sending Claire.

'Claire was there to help Jessica, she was reassuring her that everything was going to be okay. She is the one who was by her side when she died and the one who accompanied her into the spirit world.' I also explained that sometimes we're shown visions to stop events from happening, sometimes it's just to warn us so we can understand that it was going to happen no matter what.

Robbie's attitude shifted, and she started healing her grief once she realised that it was meant to be. She also drew comfort in knowing that Jessica wasn't lost in limbo. Her sister was with Jessica every step of the way on her final journey.

Accidents happen. Some children who die accidentally do end up becoming lost souls for a little while, but through prayers, psychic assistance or the intervention of Spirit, they can be rescued and crossed over to be reunited with loved ones in the spirit world. Most, however, cross over without any problem and in the days or weeks leading up to unfortunate deaths, Spirit is always by their side. They cross over in the company of love.

24
WHAT HAPPENS?

There are a lot of people like Robbie trying to come to terms with the accidental death of their beloved child. Nothing can ever make up for the void it leaves in their life, or replace the love, and I know how hard it is for some parents to move on because they simply don't know where their child has ended up.

We all know that the world is a mysterious place for children. It's partly full of wonder, joy and happiness, and partly full of uncertainty and confusion, and this is what unnerves parents. The idea that their precious child was scared during the moments leading up to their death, or that their soul is stuck in limbo, is a parent's worst nightmare. Not knowing where your child ended up is heartbreaking for some because they fear their child is lost and lonely in a strange realm and they can't reach out and touch or help them. If you have lost a child, or you know someone who has, let me shed some light on what happens. Perhaps I can help you gain a deeper understanding of what transpires when they die. And, hopefully, my words will console you.

Jessica died accidentally but she was already in good hands. Her aunt Claire was with her before she died so Jessica experienced a smooth transition to the other side. This is because there was a strong karmic potential for Jessica to die in an accident. But what happens if a child dies when it wasn't their time? Or, if it was their time, what if they decide not to cross over because they were too scared to go with their angels and guides?

Accidents are the most common reason souls become earth-bound. The accident has come on so suddenly that they are instantly separated from their body and often they don't really know what's going on. A lot of them think that they are still alive and carry on doing what they always did; however, they are living in limbo. I saw the apparition of my mother's godson after he was killed in a car accident. He came into my bedroom late one night and was trying to take refuge inside me. He did not know what was going on. A few weeks later he did manage to cross into the spirit world.

Thankfully, most children do cross over to the spirit world without a hitch, like Jessica. The transition was seamless; her aunt Claire's beautiful soul was already waiting for her, preparing her and reassuring her that there was nothing to be afraid of. When a child dies, a doorway to heaven opens up. It's a tunnel of iridescent white light that is full of peace, serenity and bliss.

In *Closer to the Light* (Bantam Books, 1990) Dr Melvin Morse tells of a study he conducted on a group of children who had survived cardiac arrest or deep comas who had a near-death experience. A near-death experience is when you have a sneak peak at the afterlife. Dr Morse discovered that most of these children reported similar near-death experiences of being outside their bodies, travelling up through a tunnel and seeing a light. Usually they saw ethereal beings waiting for them, such as spirit guides, angels and other family members who are already in spirit. These beings did not scare the kids. Whether they were in the tunnel of light, or managed to walk through the spirit world, they felt incredibly safe and happy.

What the kids saw in the spirit world varied. Some saw beautiful fields with blossom trees and ponds, just like here on earth, but everything had a luminous quality about it. Generally, they saw a familiar environment, one that was readily identified by their conscious mind so they didn't get frightened. Most saw spirits there as well.

In *Closer to the Light* Dr Morse talks about how a young girl called Katie met Elizabeth, a guide who had golden hair. This guide accompanied her up the tunnel of light and into the spirit world. Katie saw a number of spirits, including her grandfather. She also saw the souls of two young boys called Mark and Andy who were waiting to reincarnate. Despite being technically dead for a few minutes, when she was resuscitated Katie was able to provide vivid details of what was happening in her parents' home during her near-death experience and these activities were later verified.

The fascinating thing about Katie's experience is that she came from a Mormon family and therefore was not heavily indoctrinated with concepts about guardian angels and images of heaven. Although Mormons believe in Christ, they do not believe in guardian angels or spirit guides.

Drawing from experiences of children like Katie, there is a growing body of research that suggests that the soul lives on after death. I feel that this information will help parents who have lost a loved one find comfort in the knowledge that the soul is eternal.

25

JUST MISBEHAVING!

It is not uncommon for psychic kids to see lost souls. Some of their 'special friends' are lost souls. A lost soul is a spirit without a body. They live on the sideline of life because they aren't fully immersed in either the physical or spirit world. They are caught in between worlds, but this doesn't mean they are any less real or valid. These lost souls have beautiful memories and feelings just like we do. They still feel love and experience fear. And, because children who are lost souls are still kids, they can get up to a little mischief once in a while.

It was a cold winter afternoon. Soft sunbeams were cracking through the grey skies as I parked my car and walked up to Olivia's beachside apartment.

'It mostly happens in here,' she explained, as we walked into the main bedroom. Olivia is in her early twenties and extremely sensitive to energy. 'When it started a few months ago, it felt like something was following me around.'

'What exactly did you feel?' I asked.

'I felt like someone was standing behind me. I'd get a sense that I was being watched. It made me uncomfortable. I knew it wasn't my imagination. But then things started happening.'

'What things?'

'The lights in my bedroom starting switching on and off,' she said. 'And sometimes my bed starts shaking!'

I looked around the room, tuning in to see what I could pick up.

'I'm not crazy,' Olivia said, her tired eyes looking at me earnestly. I could understand where she was coming from. Imagine having this kind of paranormal activity and no one believing you. Deep down inside you are hoping to find tangible evidence to support what you are seeing.

'When does it happen? Is there any particular time?'

'No,' she said. 'It happens anytime. Sometimes I hear a racket so I go into the bedroom and then it stops.'

'What do you think it is?' I asked.

'A poltergeist,' she said adamantly. 'They're the ones who do this sort of thing.'

'Oh, do they?' I replied and sat down on the edge of the bed. 'Just because strange things are happening in here, it doesn't mean you have a poltergeist,' I explained. 'I know you think it's a dangerous spirit because it can do supernatural things and I can understand how scared you are. But the culprit here isn't a poltergeist.'

A poltergeist is a noisy lost soul, angry at being trapped on earth. Eventually their anger gives them the power to move things. But being able to move objects doesn't necessarily mean a spirit is sinister.

'What is it then? What kind of force can make my bed shake?'

'Kids,' I said.

She looked at me as if I was joking. 'Kids?'

'Yes,' I said. 'You have the souls of two little kids in here.'

'How can they do this?'

'Very easily!' I said, smiling. 'They're playing with you. They think it's a game. Every time you react to the bed shaking, they laugh. They don't mean you any harm. They're just mischievous kids playing around.'

The lost souls of children retain their childlike behaviour because they are still seeing the world the way they saw it when they were alive. No one has told them that they are dead and are now living in between worlds. So they just carry on the way they did when they were physical. As I told Olivia, 'They're just kids having fun. They don't realise that scaring you is the wrong thing to do.'

'But how did they get here?' she asked.

I spoke to the lost souls and asked them for their story.

'The two young brothers remember being in a car accident that happened near here. They walked away from it still thinking they were alive, but they couldn't find their mother. One day they decided to follow you home because you seemed like a nice person.'

'Oh, great!' Olivia didn't know how to react. All this time she had been living in fear of two playful lost souls!

'I'm going to help them cross over to the spirit world,' I explained.

I called in my spirit guides to open up an energetic tunnel of white light that acts as a doorway to the spirit world. Then I called on their mother, who had died in the accident, to come through with several angels and collect her children. She appeared as she was when she was alive, with the same beautiful smile. The only difference was that she was bathed in a radiant white light. She thanked me, then took her children by the hands and they disappeared into the tunnel of light.

'You can sleep easy tonight, Olivia,' I said.

26

IN SECRET PLACES

Olivia's visitors were having a ball in her house. I wish I could say that all lost souls had the same amount of fun, but they do not. Sometimes, a lost soul may not even make their presence known.

But if you listen carefully, you might hear them . . . the sound of footsteps, a quiet giggle, a rush of cold air brushing past you. Is it your imagination? Intuition kicks in telling you that what you are feeling is right—that you're definitely not alone.

Places, like people, are infused with personality and character but they can also have secrets. Some of the character of a place is derived from the architecture and decor; the rest of it actually comes from the vibes given off from people who hang out there. Your soul gives off a vibe that has a unique essence or feel about it. It is this energetic imprint that adds your personal touch to the atmosphere of your home, your workplace and even your belongings. The same can be said about loved ones in spirit who choose to visit from time to time, as well as earthbound souls, even those who are hanging out in secret. They also give off a vibe and, yes, you can really feel it when you are in the room with one. Discovering this fact often comes as a surprise. Many people have never joined the dots, thinking that without a body a soul can't express its personality, thoughts and feelings, let alone leave a lingering imprint of its presence.

If you have been fortunate enough to feel this kind of presence, especially if it's a loved one in spirit, then you will understand what I am talking about. Their souls give off such a strong vibe that you would swear they are there in the flesh. You may pick up on their particular brand of humour, or their compassion, maybe even smell the scent of their favourite perfume or aftershave, or hear their familiar voice. It's a beautiful and enjoyable experience because you are reconnecting with them.

However, some people get their wires crossed, and it can be difficult for them to determine whether they are picking up on the atmosphere of a place because of the way it's decorated or being influenced by residual energy left behind by others. Sometimes the vibe you are picking up on is the essence of a lost soul. If you find yourself feeling this kind of vibe in the air, why not tune in and find out who it is? Kids are especially great at picking up and exploring these kinds of vibes.

We turned up to a grand Georgian-style mansion with a huge marble portico. It had a gorgeous wisteria that draped over the extensive veranda with a profusion of lavender-coloured flowers. The staff were happy to see us.

'I'm not the only one who thinks there's a ghost here,' Marilyn told me. 'Other staff members have felt it and lately some guests have noticed a "presence".'

With me were several parapsychology students who were learning how to detect lost souls and how to help them cross over to the spirit world. As we entered the venue, most of the students couldn't see what the fuss was about. The downstairs area was exquisitely decorated in preparation for a wedding on the following day and the energy felt fantastic.

But, once we moved upstairs, things changed.

The energy got heavier and colder and a few students said that they felt a presence on the stairs, while one picked up a presence lingering in the bathroom. I knew they were spot-on and when Marilyn confirmed that these two areas were hotspots where both staff and guests had felt the ghosts, my students were happy. There were two spirits here but neither of them was malevolent; they were actually really nice lost souls. People react to the presence of a lost soul, regardless of whether it has a positive or negative vibe. It's the element of the unknown that fills them with fear. I taught my students how to clear these two lost souls by opening an energetic doorway to the spirit realm and both souls were more than happy to move on.

Then we entered a huge dilapidated dormitory.

'We don't use this wing,' explained Marilyn. 'It hasn't been used for a long while.'

We started scanning the place for lost souls, using our hands to feel the energy and our third eyes for clairvoyant visions. What distinguishes a lost soul from residual energy is this—a lost soul has consciousness, a life force energy, whereas residual energy does not. Residual energy is made up of the debris of people's thoughts and feelings.

'There's something here,' cried David. We walked over to the far corner of the room near the large windows. 'Can you feel it?'

He was right. I got the other students to tune in and they came up with impressions such as 'sad', 'lost', and 'lonely'.

'I feel like crying,' said Kerrie. 'This soul is really sad.'

That's the thing about lost souls—they still have very human emotions even though they don't have a body. Many of these souls are hidden in places where very few people can see or hear them, like this poor soul. Lost, and caught up in a time from the past, they don't know how to move on to the next world. Quite a few of them live a 'groundhog day' existence, a never-ending dream in a world tucked away from prying eyes and human interaction. These 'hidden' souls can't understand what's going on, or how to change things, so they repeat whatever feels familiar, like their favourite memory, or a game they used to play. Since time has stopped they don't have any idea of how long they've actually been playing a game or grieving over not being with their family.

I psychically tuned into the soul and saw a small boy huddled in the corner. Dressed in old-fashioned clothes, he looked totally lost, confused and frightened. It's an eye-opener for people to discover that a lot of lost souls, or ghosts, are actually more frightened of us than we are of them.

I asked my guides to show me the history of the place and they said boys had lived there and one of them, young Frederick, had died from an illness. I got images of the dormitory filled with rows and rows of beds. Frederick's bed was near the big window where we found him.

'What do you know about the history of this place?' I asked Marilyn.

'It was a rehabilitation hospital for wounded soldiers during World War Two,' she said.

I shook my head. 'I'm being shown a boarding school or orphanage; I don't see any adults, just lots of kids. Boys lived up here in these rooms. It was a dorm.'

'Oh, yes, I believe it used to be a boys' school in the 1920s,' she confirmed.

Our little hidden lost soul was a boarder who had died from an illness and never crossed over. Unlike some lost souls who venture out into the world Frederick remained within the safety of the walls in this faded dorm. His plight moved my students.

The idea that he was alone in this drab room, while downstairs there was an opulent wedding venue regularly filled with people and celebration, didn't seem fair. Marilyn had no idea that little Frederick was up there. No one did because there was no reason for staff to go into the dormitory. He was in his own little world. I soothed him by explaining what was happening, that we were there to help him go home, and he was happy because he wouldn't be lonely anymore.

It is amazing to think that a lost soul could be hidden away for more than eighty years but it can happen. Although the vast majority of children do successfully cross over to the spirit world without any problems, some slip through the cracks and become earthbound because of illness, neglect, emotional isolation or an accident or because they refuse to cross over when they see the light. These kids who are caught between worlds are still 'living' so to speak.

Even the most sceptical adult can have a huge shift in awareness when they encounter the presence of a child who is a lost soul. Helping them to move on to the spirit world is a beautiful and rewarding experience that can even become life-changing.

27
COSMIC PHONE CALLS

Since the soul is eternal it means that kids in the spirit world are alive and well. They can pop in and out of the physical world whenever they feel like visiting us. If you find it difficult feeling their presence or getting messages from them, then perhaps you can consult a medium. Better still, you can develop your own mediumship skills so you can keep a lovely connection with the people you care about.

Mediums provide a fantastic networking service between you and your loved ones on the other side. They keep the link alive so that the veil of death doesn't lock you out from reaching family and friends. I like to think of our loved ones in spirit as being only a cosmic phone call away. It's as if they have moved overseas and you aren't in a position to see them again. Sure, you'll miss them, but it is easier dealing with their absence when you know that you can pick up the phone or Skype and talk with them. In a similar way you can communicate with the other side. Wouldn't it be fantastic to share your life and get updates on what they have been doing in the spirit world? I know it's not the same as giving them a physical hug but it comes pretty close.

Initially, most people find it difficult to keep this bond going because they lack confidence and doubt their ability to pick up messages from Spirit. Have you ever doubted your ability? If so, let me assure you that you can reignite it. Young kids constantly pick themselves up after making mistakes and perhaps this is why many of them make great psychics—they keep trying! Often, what breaks the link between you and Spirit is your own conscious mind. You might tell yourself, 'I want to stay open,' but underlying fears and doubts end up shredding your confidence. Maybe old beliefs make you waver and, without realising it, you have put up a psychic block?

Many kids have mediumship abilities. They may only ever use it once in their lives, or they might surprise you by working with their channel on a regular basis. The one thing for sure is that they can seize the opportunity to talk to the people we have loved and lost. They don't have to put on a show like adult mediums, but they are often just as impressive. If you have ever watched a medium performing on stage, or visited one in person, you will know that the messages they deliver usually bring joy and peace. You never hear a spirit passing on a message saying, 'God, this place is the pits!' Those who have crossed over properly into the spirit world are really happy where they are, and the thousands of messages delivered by mediums are a testament to that. I especially love it when parents get messages from their child who is in spirit.

Recently, Carly brought her fifteen-year-old daughter Samantha to sit in on a mediumship group that I facilitate. Samantha has pronounced psychic abilities and I felt it was appropriate for her to attend this class for the night to further her understanding.

During class I sensed the presence of a new spirit who came to join us. I asked the students to tune in and write down any messages they received. When they completed the task, I asked them for feedback.

'It's a boy that I knew,' Samantha said. She looked at the other students to see if anyone could support what she was picking up.

'Yes, I got a teenage boy,' said Mary Jane. 'Was he still at school when he died? I'm getting that he was about sixteen.'

'He was a close school friend,' Samantha confirmed.

'I got that his name started with an M,' said Ken.

'He's telling me he died in a car accident,' Mary Jane added.

Samantha's eyes lit up in surprise. They were picking up on her friend Mitchell. She turned to her mother and said, 'It's Mitchell. I know it's him because I feel his vibe. It's the same energy I have been feeling in my bedroom lately. I know he has been trying to contact me. I didn't know what to do to connect with him properly so I kind of talk to him from my mind.'

Samantha got the validation she needed to prove that she wasn't imagining things.

I also got confirmation. 'Mitchell needs you to tell his mother that he wasn't doing anything stupid, that the accident wasn't his fault. It just happened but he is now okay,' I said. 'Oh, and he is also telling her that he really likes that she's kept his room untouched but he is happy for her to let other people stay there now.'

'Wow, that's awesome. He told me that I should talk to his mother,' Samantha said.

For Samantha, knowing that Mitchell was still able to talk with her took away the pain of his loss and opened up a new level of awareness. She knew her psychic ability was real and she felt she could put it to good use by helping other people.

Two days later I heard from Samantha. She told me that she shared the mediumship messages about Mitchell with other kids. She also gave Mitchell's mother his message and it made such a huge difference to her. His mother told Samantha that only the day before she had been sitting on Mitchell's bed debating with herself whether or not she should let other people use his room.

Samantha is a medium in the making. Her forte is talking to Spirit. As she develops this psychic skill, Samantha will be able to provide a valuable 'linking in' service from Spirit to families to help them keep that cosmic phone line open.

The joy of getting a cosmic phone call from a child who is in spirit is beyond words. Parents who have been fortunate enough to go through this experience will tell you that it is a peak moment in their lives. The marvel of having a medium connect the line is a gift many have been praying for ever since their child passed away. This bridge to heaven opens a pathway to communicating with their child anytime they want.

There has been a seismic shift in awareness towards mediumship and more and more people are taking advantage of this service. Although I do mediumship work myself, occasionally I like to watch other mediums because I love seeing how an audience responds to receiving messages. When I was given a free ticket to watch a well-known medium, I couldn't wait. He came on stage and spent an hour giving people a spiritual lecture, which I feel is valuable because it helps an audience understand what loved ones are doing while they are in the spirit world. Then he began channelling messages from spirits.

At one point he announced (I am paraphrasing here), 'I have the soul of a newborn baby boy here.' The medium walked to the other side of the stage, pointing to a small section of the audience to the right. 'The message is for someone over here. Baby wants to talk with his mother. I'm getting the letter S . . .' He paused for a moment as he tuned in to get more clarification. 'S . . . I feel her name is something like Simone.'

The audience was quiet, hanging on to every word. 'He says he had problems with his heart. I'm being shown that there was something wrong, that it wasn't developed properly, it's like it was back to front.'

A young woman in the audience put up her hand. 'That's my son, Nicholas,' she said tearfully.

'Nicholas is telling me that the doctors had no option but to operate,' the medium said. 'He was only a few days old.'

His grieving mother listened intently as the medium explained how happy Nicholas was in spirit, and how he was visiting her regularly and knew what she was going through. Nicholas wanted her to know that he was only meant to be here for a few days because he was having a 'test drive' of what it's like being physical again. And that he would return to her in a few years by reincarnating back into her family.

Like many parents who have lost a child, Simone worried about what happened to her child's soul. It is one thing for a friend to say, 'Hey, they are okay,' to comfort and reassure you, but when a total stranger gives you intimate details about your child, things like their character, or what happened when they were young, how they died and what they are doing now, it's so much easier to accept.

And you know that the cosmic telephone line has really opened up for you. There's a sense of freedom and empowerment that comes from knowing that their spirit is happy. It is also reassuring to know that you can reach across the veil anytime you want.

28

TELL THEM TO GO

Children turn to their parents for reassurance. Whether they're having difficulties at school or they have fallen down and grazed their knees, they reach out to be comforted. All they want is a pair of warm arms wrapped around them and to hear the words, 'Everything is going to be all right'. It's easy for parents to perform this role when they know what to expect and what to do. But what happens when you are out of your depth? Sometimes an unsettling paranormal encounter catches you out. Isn't it better to have some knowledge about Spirit, especially if you have a psychic child? At least you will be equipped to handle the unexpected.

Sixteen-year-old Stevie went to bed with her pet and best friend, a fox terrier named Ella. One night she couldn't sleep because she got a weird, but familiar, sensation that somebody was watching her. Stevie had never experienced this sensation at night before, only on the odd occasion during the day when saw coloured figures.

For as long as she could remember Stevie saw spirits in different colours. As a child, she relied on the colours to determine their intentions. Bright and clear colours meant that they were nice; dark colours meant that they were angry or disruptive spirits.

'I decided not to open my eyes, thinking this way I could ignore the spirit in my bedroom,' she said. 'I was sick of dealing with my physic abilities.'

I can appreciate Stevie's point of view. At times it can be overwhelming having to deal with this sort of stuff when you don't fully understand what is going on.

'I was scared,' she admitted. 'I convinced myself that if I told myself nothing was there, it would go away. But it didn't work. It only made it worse. I could feel a presence moving closer towards me and I was trembling with fear.'

Then she felt someone poking her arm. 'It was an extremely hard poke. I knew this spirit wanted my attention, but I didn't want to deal with it. I had no idea how to communicate with them, or how to protect myself. My immediate reaction was to pull my quilt way over my head and hide under it.'

I perfectly understand this response. I reacted the same way myself the first time I saw my spirit guide hovering over me.

'I was terrified, so I tried not to make any noise,' Stevie said. 'Ten minutes later the spirit was getting desperate to be noticed. I heard an extremely loud clap and my dog yelped. I lifted the quilt and saw Ella leap across the room and into the wardrobe. Then I saw it. A tall black figure was standing in the corner of my room.'

Stevie's initial reaction was to think that her brother was playing a joke on her. She said, 'Ryan, this isn't funny anymore, get out of my room.' Instead the figure started coming towards her and she intuitively realised it wasn't her brother. The spirit got closer and she noticed that it had no face.

'I got the feeling it was a teenage girl,' said Stevie. 'The girl was walking towards my bed, and then she crawled on top of it. I started screaming and kicking the quilt off.'

'Somebody is in my room!' she yelled as she ran to her parents' bedroom to get her mum. She knew her mother would be able to get rid of the girl.

Stevie's mum Diane initially thought that there was a real intruder in her daughter's room. She sent Stevie's dad to check, while she tried to calm Stevie down so she could explain what had happened. Once Diane realised that it was a spirit, she went in and cleansed the room. She used white light to clear negative energies left by the lost soul. Diane then called on her spirit guides to open a doorway to help the girl's spirit cross to the spirit world. After the energy in the room settled down, Diane told Stevie it was safe to go back to bed, but Stevie refused to sleep in there. She asked her father to stay there instead.

The next day Stevie's arm felt sore so she checked it and discovered a large blue bruise where the girl had poked her. The spirit was real!

Diane explained to Stevie that she was like a lighthouse to spirits because she was psychically aware. 'Your aura is bright and the spirit of a lost soul sees this and thinks that they've finally found someone who will be able to see and help them.'

Then Diane taught Stevie how to energetically protect herself, and how to seal off her bedroom so she wouldn't have this problem again. Stevie learnt how to put up a beautiful cocoon of white light around her, followed by a lovely golden light to protect her aura.

She used a tornado of white light to sweep through her bedroom to cleanse away disruptive energies, and a golden light to energetically seal and protect the space.

Things have improved since then.

'Occasionally, a lost soul still manages to get into my room,' Stevie said, 'but I know I can get Mum to clear them and cross them back into the spirit world. Mum explained that my guides let these lost souls in because they need my help to find their way back home. I know I'm psychic and I can do this too, but I'm not confident enough yet. Sometimes I try to tell myself that I'm only imagining what I am sensing but when I hear spirits talking aloud to me, and see the colours around them, I know it is real . . . very real.'

You can help your child overcome their fears of the supernatural by explaining what spirits are. Assure them that you will help them deal with the problem. It is important to them to know that they don't have to go it alone, that they always have you there to help them no matter what.

29
THE FAIRY KINGDOM

There is a misconception that the supernatural world is a frightening place full of ghouls and ghosts. That's like saying the earth is full of malevolent people when the truth is that it is a mixture of unconditionally loving souls and some not-so-loving souls. The supernatural world also has its fair share of beautiful and loving souls and even mythical beings.

A child's imagination is a rich playground where mythical creatures and magical fairy kingdoms are real. As adults we may enjoy the fantasy genre but we always know where to draw the line between fiction and reality. Or do we? My guides have shown me worlds within worlds. They coexist side by side but in different dimensions. One of these spirit realms is called the Devic Kingdom. *Deva* is a Sanskrit word that literally translates as 'shining ones' and it can apply equally to nature spirits, angels and lofty archangels. A lot of adults shut out this other world but kids love exploring it. They especially interact with nature spirits so I will focus on these spritely little beings.

One of my favourite stories when I was a child was about the apple tree fairy who decided to take a vacation during spring because she wanted to be lazy. As a result the tree didn't blossom. In its simplistic way the story was trying to get the message across that the natural world is aided by the spirit world. You will have noticed that folklore is full of stories of gnomes, goblins, leprechauns, fairies and other-worldly beings that live beyond our periphery. Most adults think of them as characters from children's books and that there is no truth behind them. Kids might argue this point. The Devic Kingdom is full of spirits that act as nature's helpers. They're not individualised like we are; they share group consciousness and they work as a whole, just as bees and ants work together as a collective.

The most fundamental nature spirits are the elemental spirits, called 'form builders', that look after the elements of earth, water, fire and air. These wispy energy beings are the spiritual essence of the elements. They are known as the gnomes (earth), undines (water), salamanders (fire) and sylphs (air). Lots of people have cement garden gnomes and perhaps some have heard tales of the gnomes and how they dig the earth. But the cute little garden statues don't look anything like the elemental gnome which is a brightly coloured wisp of conscious energy. These elemental spirits have a job which is to work at an atomic level with the soil and this work helps plants to grow. Similarly, undines work with water, salamanders with the transformational energy of fire, and sylphs with the air and wind. Occasionally you might catch one in the corner of your eye as they shoot past you.

The elementals get their orders from angels, and they generally do as they're told without question. They are sometimes considered playful and 'mischievous', or even dangerous, because they take orders indiscriminately. Elementals don't just listen to devas, they listen to your thoughts and feelings and respond accordingly. If you wish for something lovely to happen to someone, the elementals race around trying to make this happen. Likewise, they'll add their energy to a negative thought. They also play a part in alchemy and magic. So they're not really responsible if they do create a little mayhem because their role is to 'do' not to 'question'.

The next level of devas are the nature spirits (which some people call fairies) who look after the plant and animal kingdoms. Plants and animals have their own consciousness. Sure, it's different to ours, but they still have consciousness. They have their own spirit and this is why they have their own guardian angels in the form of nature spirits. They are looking after your plants right now. These devas also include some of the mythical beings in folklore, such as dragons who look after the earth's electromagnetic energy. They're not physical but are energetic beings that can be called on to help manifest changes in the natural environment.

It's fantastic that psychic kids love to explore the Devic Kingdom. A student of mine called Ariana loved playing with fairies as a child.

'I went looking under toadstools for fairies, literally!' said Ariana. 'Our backyard was full of them. I used to run around looking for fairies and I would see them—beautiful wisps of gorgeous-coloured beings near the rose bushes and around the peach tree. I lost all track of time while I was playing with them. Well, I was in their world.'

'How did it feel?' I asked.

'Great. I felt like I stepped into a magical world where I could be whatever I wanted. My fairy friends showed me how they lived. I talked to them, followed them, and lost myself in a timeless place where it didn't matter who I was. It was so much fun! When my mother called for me to come in for dinner, I would yell out, "Not yet please, I'm with the fairies."'

Kids today are spending less time in gardens. Apartment living, homework, computers, the internet, mobile phones and busy parents . . . it seems such a shame that they're not out there letting their imaginations go wild while they explore this hidden world of elemental beings. If you do have a garden, why not spend some time with your child talking to the nature spirits that look after your plants and let them tell you their story. Ask them to help your flowers, vegetables and trees to grow, or call on them to protect wildlife like birds that find their way into your backyard. If you do live in an apartment, you could go to the park or into a forest and help your child search for fairies. It could end up being a magical day!

30
IT'S PERFECTLY NATURAL

Tristan has it, and so do many psychic kids—a real affinity for nature, much like our ancestors. It is a connection to the earth that many adults are slowly realising has been missing in their lives. Our modern world doesn't always provide scope for kids to explore nature. City living, parents working long hours, computer games, and always having so much to do mean that we don't often have the opportunity to get into nature. But exploring nature's hidden depths can teach children so much about the web of life, as Ethan found out.

By the time he was able to walk Ethan was whizzing around the backyard exploring plants and trees and looking under rocks for bugs and other fascinating creatures. By the age of four his empathy with nature was obvious to his mother.

Ethan is now a precocious sixteen-year-old. There is clarity in his blue eyes that draws you in and you know you are talking to a unique and spiritually evolved teenager. I asked him to describe his experiences and he revealed that from a young age he was 'curious about how things worked, how things lived and how everything was connected'.

His mother understood and encouraged his development. 'She helped me to unlock my purpose here on earth,' he said. 'I remember when I was five I knew how to heal my mother. I didn't think about what I was doing, I just knew how to use colours and where to place my hands on her. I would think positive thoughts that would help heal her and let the energy come through me.'

When Ethan was eleven he was doing spell work and began developing what he describes as a 'bond with the four basic elements'. That is, the elements earth, water, fire and air.

'How did you feel it?' I asked, curious to know how a child relates to elements.

'I felt the earth beneath me and the rushing of the waves, I felt the flicker of the flame and the whistling of the wind.' Mature beyond his years, Ethan recognised that our earth is our womb and by relating to the elements he began to understand this link.

'One day, when I was about fourteen, I heard the whispers of shrubs in the country,' he told me. 'So I decided to learn to communicate with the trees, specifically those with whom I felt a connection. I heard their deep voices and understood their messages.'

I immediately understood what he was talking about, because my own son Tristan had connected with and talked to distressed trees. Kids can really link into nature as a living, breathing being.

It has consciousness and if you open up you can feel it in the elements around you, just like Ethan.

'How do you explore this connection?' I asked him.

'In meditations,' he replied. 'When I meditated I felt the urge to feel my heartbeat with my hand, and to slow my breathing. I heard the voice of Mother Earth, and since then she has blessed me with her words of wisdom, her meditations, her presence, her energy and her love.'

'Did the voice tell you what to do?'

'No. I was allowed to know the truth and make my own decisions. Sometimes getting two-way answers can be frustrating,' he admitted. 'But I have learnt to live with that.'

Over the past few years Ethan he has come up with innovative ideas and concepts about our link with nature. While he has been influenced and supported by his family, and he has adapted some of his healing ideas from watching his mother do reiki healing rituals, most of his knowledge is derived from his sixth sense.

Ethan has opened up to working with his spirit guides and has learnt that one of the reasons he was born was to 'protect the earth'. Initially, he felt a little overwhelmed by the idea of having to protect the planet.

'I didn't know how I could complete that task in my lifetime,' he said thoughtfully.

'Did you find the answer?' I asked.

'Yes, I meditated and delved into myself, and spoke to my guides. They told me that I was under no obligation to fulfil this goal, unless I really wanted to do it.'

This took the burden off his shoulders. Ethan understood that things would unravel as they needed to and he would know what to do when the time was right.

The most important thing for Ethan is that he has a support network to help him on his journey to discover his talent and to use it in a positive way to help the environment.

'I have a friend, Jenny, who's pretty awesome and really gifted. I can talk to her about things I sense because we can connect on the same level and we have the same talents. We've even done some meditations together at school in the lunch hour on the back oval,' he said with a grin.

Ethan also added, 'I think growing up in a household where it's normal to work with my psychic self makes me feel good. I know I have definite gifts that I can draw on.'

He has also joined a colour therapy/energetic healing circle, which gave him the opportunity to further communicate with the earth.

Late last year Ethan began feeling an immense desire to fulfil his mission. Ethan sees the earth as a conduit of the realms, where all dimensions are actually blended and are able to be accessed. He described this feeling as encompassing a 'perfect balance, a combination of masculine and feminine, making a perfect midpoint. It's like the sun, and the moon, are two poles, and my work is the midpoint between them.'

'I see it clearly,' he said with conviction. 'I am here to help Mother Earth fight back. Without her we can't exist. So I am here to preserve her and her creations, those innocent and those different, yet all the same.'

Perhaps you have noticed the rise in environmental awareness in the youth of today? They are concerned with the state of the environment and really do want to make a difference.

I call Ethan a 'spiritual warrior', one of the many evolved souls that are being born across the planet to usher in much-needed changes in awareness of how we treat the earth and how we can work to make it a better place for all.

On a final note I thought I would mention that a local member of parliament and a local radio station have taken a liking to Ethan. They are encouraging him to go on radio and talk about his abilities and views on life. There's a definite path that the universe is showing him, by supporting and helping him to become all that he can be. It is also showing him that there is increasing interest in the community for all things psychic.

31

THAT FLOATING FEELING

Psychic phenomena are much more widespread than most people realise, regularly spilling into everyday events. They are usually dismissed as 'one of those things'. You might give it scant regard because you don't understand it, or know how to classify it, so you simply ignore it or let it go without further investigation. Things like having an out-of-body experience, which should get most people thinking, are usually shaken off with excuses like 'I must have dreamt it' or 'I must have imagined it'.

An out-of-body experience, or OBE, is the sensation of slipping out of your body. It is a common psychic experience, even if it is brief, that everyone will probably experience at one stage in life. It usually occurs as you are starting to fall asleep and can also happen when you are in a deep meditative state. Has your child ever talked about looking down at themselves from above? If they have, then they have experienced the most common out-of-body sensation.

A migraine hit me late one spring afternoon when I was twelve so I took myself to bed. I didn't like taking painkillers so lay down and closed my eyes. I don't know how long I was there for. The pain was so bad I couldn't think clearly. I remember hearing laughter outside the bedroom window from my sisters who were playing hopscotch on the driveway. I wanted to be out there playing too, anything was better than being curled up in a foetal position with my hands cradling my head and wishing the pain would just leave.

Then something strange happened. I felt myself slipping out of my body and the next thing I knew I was floating up to the ceiling. I didn't know what was happening. I was floating above myself. I could see my body and remember thinking, 'Wow, I feel free and liberated!' No fear coursed through me, just an exhilarating feeling of lightness that defied words. I wondered if I was dreaming, but it didn't feel like a dream because I was consciously wide awake and I could hear my sisters outside. I was out of my body, in a sort of limbo that I couldn't explain.

Moments later I felt my body shuddering and I knew I was back in it. I wasn't in two places at once anymore. I looked around me and I was still in my bedroom, it was still afternoon, and the sound of my sisters laughing still wafted through the open window. Sitting up, I realised that my splitting headache had magically disappeared. Without thinking anything more about the experience, I ran outside to play.

Even though it was a weird experience I did not share it with anyone else. It never occurred to me to tell someone. And, like me, lots of kids neglect to tell their parents and friends about these kinds of experiences. I did not know that having an out-of-body experience was something extraordinary yet perfectly natural for kids to experience. Eventually, as I had more and more out-of-body experiences, I came to realise that they were telling me that my body was not who I was, that there was a part of me that could move in and out of it. I discovered my soul had a level of freedom that my body, which was confined to the three-dimensional world, could never achieve. My soul could fly above me, pop over to visit a friend and could even jump into different realms of reality.

Most out-of-body experiences are fascinating; some are fun because you get to fly around a room! Occasionally, you might feel unsettled because you find it hard reintegrating back into your body after an out-of-body experience. The astral body has returned but it has not fully realigned back into your soul and physical body. If your child tells you that they woke up from their sleep but they could not move their limbs, or they were calling out and no one could hear them, it is because they have not realigned properly. And since quite a lot of out-of-body experiences are spontaneous, it catches them unexpectedly.

Explain what is happening to them in terms that they can understand. You can also teach them this simple exercise to use whenever they feel unsettled because of an out-of-body experience.

Tell them not to be scared when it happens. Assure them that they can remedy the situation by first stating their intention, 'I am back in my body,' and then focusing on feeling their fingers. Then get them to focus on trying to wiggle their fingers. It may take a minute or two but while they are focusing on this task it keeps their mind occupied so fear is held at bay. Assure them that the more they try to wiggle their fingers, and focus on realigning, the faster it will happen. Soon they will snap out of it and be back in sync with their body.

Out-of-body experiences can also happen when your child is day-dreaming. This is literally when they have their heads in the clouds! They become so relaxed and lost in their imagination, dreaming of things to come, their astral body sometimes projects out. There is nothing unusual in this; it is a form of splitting consciousness, and their awareness is in two places at once. Their body is here in the physical while their astral body, a part of their soul, is off wandering in the astral realm, which is an energetic world of endless possibilities and potential. It is where they go naturally during sleep. Daydreaming is a source of inspiration, a powerful tool to help them manifest the things they want in life. Not only does it give them a welcome break from the mundane aspects of life, it gives them a wonderful platform to think about new ideas, explore and create.

When Tristan was twelve his favourite Xbox game was a car rally and the car he preferred to use in the game was a classic Volvo 240. He constantly daydreamed about owning his own Volvo 240, imagining himself behind the steering wheel. Then when he turned seventeen a white Volvo 240 was bequeathed to his step-mother. Tristan bought his dream car for a song!

A daydream is a form of creative visualisation. So, really, when you're daydreaming you're taking one of the first steps towards manifesting the things you want in life. Every time you visualise yourself doing something, you're creating an energy matrix for future events within the astral realm. The adage 'As above, so below' comes into play. What is created energetically through thoughts, feelings and visions in the astral realm can become tangible and real in your life.

When your child daydreams they are at the threshold of new discoveries, and it can give them the foundation of things to come. Go on, encourage those daydreams!

32

THE MONSTER
DID IT!

Children's imaginations leave no stone unturned. That's part of their appeal. Yet, it can land them in hot water, especially when they lose the boundary between what's real and what's not. A lively imagination is such a beautiful asset when it works within a specific framework but it can cause confusion and chaos for parents. This is especially so when a child makes up stories about paranormal experiences. While most kids are very truthful, some create the most incredible stories which can throw their parents off track and even create fear and anxiety. When a child tells you they are seeing spirits, how do you know it is the truth?

Being discerning is put to the test when a child's imagination is running amok. They are known to add a few colourful untruths to the mix, especially if it means escaping discipline, and it's

137

understandable why parents scratch their heads and say, 'Which side is up?'

We have all heard the line 'the monster did it' and seen the huge swell of tears in their big eyes when they know they have been caught out. It can be hard for parents to determine when a child is telling the truth when they venture into the paranormal realm. Did little Johnny really see a spirit? Is Katie just making this up to fool me? Kids are impressionable. They are very open to suggestion, and with minds like sponges they don't miss a trick. Sometimes they make up things because it sounds good. They may have picked an idea up from watching television, or heard others talk about it, then they decide it would be fun to imagine it. They play-act it out. Most parents want to do the right thing by their kids but when they are carrying on about spirits sitting by the bed, or say things like 'Grandma's here,' it's easy to understand why parents don't want to buy into that reality. Firstly, your child has demonstrated the range of their fantastic imagination over the years, and secondly, you don't have the tools to tune in and *see* if what they are saying is true.

I have had a few concerned parents bring their child in to see me to 'test' them, so to speak, because their child is claiming to be talking to a strange person in the house. The parents themselves don't sense anything and they want to make sure that they are doing the right thing before dismissing the claims or disciplining their child for telling lies.

When Julia arrived with five-year-old blond-haired Jordan, the first thing he did was to shoot me an inquiring look that said, 'I'm assessing you'. Then he sat down, adopting a guarded stance, as his mother explained her concerns about the number of spirits he had seen and the messages he was getting.

The child was gifted, there was no doubt. But I could see that he was clever enough to spice up his experiences.

I asked him to describe who was standing next to me. He pointed out that I had a male spirit guide, and this was true. Then he stated that I had a strange creature around me, going into detail. His concerned mother looked on, totally out of her depth.

We ran a few other tests before I asked Jordan to sit in the reception area while I talked to his mother for a few minutes. I explained that Jordan was psychic, but he also let his imagination run wild, especially regarding the creature.

His mother was stumped. What was she supposed to do?

I gave Julia this advice: When Jordan tells you what he sees, trust in your own instinct. Does it ring true? Don't listen to logic. What do you feel? What kind of vibe is Jordan giving off when he is talking to you about his experience?

The energy of his aura will reflect the differences. If he is talking his truth, his aura will be vibrant and open. When is making something up, or trying to convince himself he sees something that's not there, his energies will feel a little blocked, and his solar plexus chakra will be overextended. The solar plexus is the empowerment chakra, and when someone is trying to control or manipulate a situation, or attempt to make themselves feel larger than life by imagining things, then the energy will be overextended. This means that the energy from the solar plexus will rush out past the spiritual body.

I taught Julia how to feel his energy, and how to feel the solar plexus chakra. I showed her a balanced solar plexus, training her to follow the vortex of energy from the centre of the chakra just under the diaphragm and out to the spiritual body. Then I showed her how far an overextended chakra flows by placing her hand near the

sternum again. I asked her to feel the energy. If there was a weak
pulse then the chakra was blocked. Then I asked her to place her
hand just past the spiritual body (about an arm's length away from
the sternum) and asked her to feel the energy. If the energy felt
like a strong breeze that pushed her hand out, then the chakra was
definitely overextended.

You can learn techniques like this to help you evaluate whether
or not your child is telling the truth or if their imagination is in
overdrive. It will help you discern what's real and what isn't, so
you don't overreact or get anxious, and help you address the issue,
especially if their imagination is playing up. It also gives them a
clear message that you can tell the difference and this will help
create a healthy boundary. When your child imagines things, you
can respond accordingly; and when they are being psychic, you
can support their reality.

Setting healthy boundaries will give you peace of mind.
Because it helps you call the right shots, your child will never feel
unheard, confused or angry because the two of you are on different pages.

33
STAR

When you tune into your child, you will intuitively know whether they are rambling on about something real or imagined. Kids like to play-act what they want to be when they grow up. Surprisingly, many of them have the knack of play-acting the very job or role they eventually adopt as adults.

When I was a kid I told people I was going to be a writer. Some dismissed it, others laughed and a few paid attention to my aspiration. But there was no doubt about it in my mind — I knew that my daydream of becoming a writer was based on my soul truth. I never questioned my vision. I simply knew what was in my heart, what my soul urge was. The psychic part of me sensed that this was the path that was right for me. And it was. That dream came true.

This is why I urge parents to keep a lookout for their kids' intuitive role-playing because it may be their guiding star to the person they will become. It is the star that shines most brightly for them;

the soul light that guides them on their karmic path. They are born with a smouldering ember deep within them that inspires them to move along certain paths. They have an incredible knack for identifying and feeding their aspirations. Yes, I know that not all kids have this sensation, but most do.

I was talking to my sister Frances the other day about this chapter for the book and how I wanted a few stories on kids who followed their soul's star. She looked at me and grinned.

'Follow me,' she said, leading me out of the kitchen towards the hall. 'You've got to see this.'

We stepped into her teenage daughter Olivia's room and opened the wardrobe. On the timber panel were a few precious childhood photos. The one that jumped out immediately was of Olivia when she was about four years old. She was dressed in a white doctor's outfit and had a stethoscope around her neck and toy first-aid kit in her hand. And, the biggest, cheesiest grin that said, 'Yes, I know what I am doing.'

'You know Livy always loved nursing and playing doctors,' Frances said proudly.

She was right. For as long as I can remember Olivia has wanted to work in paediatrics but I had forgotten how she dressed the part and role-played when she was a young child.

'Livy loved this outfit,' Frances continued. 'She was always wearing it. Whenever I got sick, she would play nurse, take my pulse, give me water and try to make me feel better. But it was more than play-acting. She kept telling me that she was going to grow up and be a doctor or nurse and look after little kids. She's always known what she wanted to be when she grew up. She's never waivered.'

Knowing what she wants to be inspires and motivates Olivia to achieve her goal of working in paediatrics. She studies hard because she wants to keep that dream alive. Her star is shining, its bright light paving the way for her. And I have no doubt that she will do it. I tuned in psychically and saw that this will happen, and I even looked at her numerology and astrology chart and it is all there in her karmic blueprint. Olivia is in perfect sync with where her soul wants her to be.

Other parents I've spoken with share similar stories of how their kids instinctively knew what they wanted to be. Their souls are already imprinted with karmic information that triggers moments of insight and inspiration to guide them along their path.

What about your child? Do they know what they want to be? It's great if they do. But how can you help a child who doesn't know what they want to be? Why not give them a helping hand by getting them to do a quick little meditation I call 'Follow My Star'.

Get them to relax by concentrating on their breathing until you can see that they are settled. When they are ready, ask them to imagine themselves standing under the Milky Way on a bright moonlit evening. Get them to choose a star in the sky that is shining brightly. Once they have chosen a star, ask them to make a wish upon that star. Tell them to repeat the words, 'Show me what I am going to be when I grow up.' Allow a few minutes to do this.

Now, ask them to visualise the star floating down from the sky until it is shining above their head, the star sending a flood of beautiful light in front of them. Ask them if they can see a vision of themselves as a grown-up dressed in the outfit for their job or in the environment of their job. Give them about five minutes to explore this future.

When they have finished, ask them to put their wish into the star and see it floating back up into the Milky Way. Once they have done that, tell them to take a few deep breaths and then open their eyes.

You can ask them to share their vision with you if they want to. If they didn't see anything, tell them that's okay and that you can try again another day and eventually it will come to them.

Your psychic child's soul knows that it was born with a purpose, a role to play in the tapestry of life. By being open to their day-dreams and play-acting, you can help them to bring their vision to fruition.

34
FAIRYTALES

Inspiration comes from deep within the soul. The spiritual body, which is the outer layer of the aura, holds our 'potential to be' so it is like a pool of unrealised dreams waiting to unfold. It also understands our karma, the lessons in life we need to experience to enrich our lives.

Every so often, your child's soul lets them in on a secret. The spiritual body releases a secret about one of their life's themes. And it is unveiled in a clever way . . . through fairytales!

Did you know that fairytales can divulge an idea or lesson your child will experience at some point? It might last for months or years, and even influence them for decades. And most people do not even know that their fairytale is playing in the backstage of their awareness.

A few years ago I asked my metaphysics students to write down their favourite fairytale. It raised a few eyebrows.

'Why?' asked Dai.

'You'll see,' I said enigmatically.

Once they finished the task they still looked baffled.

'I want you to think about the fairytale you picked. Why did you pick that fairytale out of all the fairytales you've read? There's a reason.' Then I revealed my favourite fairytale was The Swan Princess.

'So you wanted to be a princess?' Anne asked.

'Not exactly,' I said. 'Listen to the story then I'll explain.'

The Swan Princess is the story of a princess called Elisa. Her wicked stepmother placed a magical spell on Elisa's eleven brothers. They were forced to leave the kingdom to live as swans by day and humans from midnight to dawn. Then she banished Elisa.

Elisa's swan brothers rescued her and took her to a foreign land where she befriended the queen of the fairies. The fairy queen told Elisa that she could break the curse on her brothers by gathering nettles that grew around the graveyard and knitting them to make shirts to place over the swans. However, while she was doing this, she had to take a vow of silence. If she uttered a single word before she completed the eleven shirts, her brothers would die.

One day a king rode past Elisa and immediately fell in love with her. He gave her a room at his castle where she could continue knitting. But others weren't happy. They judged her because she was different. They thought she was a witch because of her activities, especially when she was found by the graveyard collecting nettles, and put her on trial for witchcraft. Desperate to finish the shirts Elisa carried on her work despite the jeers of the crowd as she was being carted to the place where she was to be executed.

Suddenly the eleven swans descended on her and she managed to get the shirts on all of them except for one. The last shirt was still missing one sleeve. Magically the brothers were returned to their human form, except the eleventh brother who retained one swan wing. They revealed their story and Elisa was set free and reunited with her brothers.

'But you're not a witch!' said Mary.

'No,' I said, laughing. 'But I identified with that story the most when I was a kid for a reason. My soul knew that I would have lessons along this line. It is my archetypal story and it played out in my life especially when I started teaching metaphysics. People were judging me and I also spent a lot of time serving others even though silently I endured my own personal pain. My lesson was to remain dedicated and strong enough to withstand the challenges.'

At the time I was still working incredibly long hours despite being unwell. I was still playing out the Swan Princess archetype without realising it. But, just like Princess Elisa, I persevered.

The next day Chiara and I took a quick walk around the small lake near our home. Each spring a pair of black swans returned to nest there. It was summer now and the cygnets were getting larger. Walking down the south end of the lake, we noticed a grey-downed cygnet was trapped in a small area fenced off by logs. It couldn't get back into the water.

'We've got to help it,' said Chiara. 'What if a dog comes past?'

I looked around but couldn't see any dogs.

I tried to approach the distressed cygnet but it resisted me, it even tried to bite me. Several minutes passed. Suddenly Chiara's tone grew urgent. 'Hurry, there's a big black dog coming. It's not on a leash.'

I looked up and 50 metres away a dog was fast approaching us. I struggled to catch the cygnet but finally gathered it in my arms, carried it over the log fence and got it back to the lake and its family—just before the dog arrived.

Then it hit me. Didn't I talk about the Swan Princess last night? Here I was rescuing again, and this time it was a baby swan. Talk about synchronicity!

The lesson of my fairytale was to realise the power of endurance. Once I learnt this lesson, things changed and people stopped judging me and began accepting my work as well.

What is your favourite childhood fairytale? What fairytale does your child like? Pay attention to the fairytale because it will reveal something that your child's soul already knows — a life lesson.

Kids are drawn to stories that they can relate to. They see themselves in the story because it reflects a karmic lesson their soul is here to learn. Remarkably, every adult I have used my 'fairytale therapy' on discovered that their favourite fairytale actually did play out in their lives. Go on, release your inner child and step into the wonderful world of fairytales. You might be surprised by what you find.

35
I'M NOT SCARED

I know Tristan and Chiara's imaginations aren't in overdrive when they tell me that see spirits. I know they can see a lot of activity but I also know that this alone doesn't define their ability. They have a broad range of psychic skills and they are slowly learning how to master them. So I find it a little surprising that some people automatically expect psychic kids to panic when they see a spirit, and feel they must automatically shoo all ghostly apparitions away.

Thankfully, my kids seek the help of their spirit guides or open up and talk to me about their concerns so I can help them understand them. Like my kids, a great number of psychic kids have the good sense to 'feel' the truth instead of reacting to an apparition. Are they dealing with a restless ghost or a benevolent being? Does the energy feel good or bad? And how can they tell the difference?

We were on a shoot to film paranormal activity at a house which happened to back on to a cemetery (a cliché, I know). Tristan, his girlfriend Jade and school friends Sam and Matt had offered to play roadies for directors Eli and Tony and to carry equipment.

Ruth, who lived in the house, was troubled by a paranormal presence that had the knack of switching lights on and off in the middle of the night. After years of putting up with these disturbing antics, she had decided it was okay to bring someone in to handle the ghost. But she also wanted answers. Who was in her house? Why were they hanging around? Why wouldn't they go when she told them to?

I was standing in the main bedroom ready to tune in and see what I could find when Tristan walked in to ask me a question.

Out of the blue, Tony said, 'Tristan, are you psychic as well?'

'Oh, I pick up things,' Tristan replied.

This was a surprising admission as Tristan wasn't in the habit of telling people about his abilities. My children never openly advertise what I do for a living. When they were younger and wanting to fit in with groups, they thought my line of work was 'too out there' and didn't like to talk about it. Instead they would respond to questions with vague replies like, 'Oh, my parents work for themselves'.

Turning to me, Tony asked if Tristan could be filmed separately from me to see what he could pick up by himself. It would also be interesting to compare our findings. Tristan loved the idea and boldly stepped forward, his palms outstretched and his eyes closed, and tuned in while I slipped out of the room to give him the space he needed. Undeterred by the camera and director, Tristan began relaying his psychic impressions.

'I feel that there is a spirit of an older lady,' he said confidently. 'She's holding her head like she hurt herself there or she had a disease in the head that killed her. She's also limping like she has a bad leg.'

'Does she scare you?' Tony asked.

'No, no, she doesn't. She seems nice enough, her energy feels good, but there is a lot of emotion in this room. I feel she is sad.'

A lot of people automatically assume that lost souls walk around moaning and rattling chains, but the truth is that most are simple everyday people that happen to be earthbound. Tristan was comfortable, and it is important to understand that children who happen to see spirits can often feel quite comfortable with them.

I returned and Tristan left. Then I tuned in and said almost the same things as Tristan, adding that the presence in the bedroom was actually Ruth's grandmother in spirit. I also picked up that she had lived on a farm, she permanently injured her leg when she was in her twenties and she died from an injury to the brain. This validated the spirit to Ruth who confirmed these details about her grandmother.

'But why is she haunting me?' Ruth asked, confused.

'She's not a ghost, she isn't stuck in the physical world. She is in spirit. Your grandmother isn't haunting you. She has been choosing to visit you for a long time.'

'What?'

'She comes and goes on a regular basis,' I explained. 'She has been worried about you. She says that the lights started going on and off in your house when she started visiting. She's saying something about you separating from your husband at the time and that you were frightened because you had two kids to bring up and you had no support.'

'Oh my god,' she exclaimed. 'That's when the lights went really crazy. It was more than fifteen years ago!'

Back then Ruth's house was isolated. Living next to a cemetery didn't exactly thrill her or calm her fears. She was frightened of being on her own. Now, a suburb had sprung up around her but the lights were still playing up.

'But why is she still visiting?'

'She's telling me it's because you're feeling emotionally overwhelmed,' I said. Tristan had also picked this up. 'Have you noticed that the lights play up during periods when you are feeling sad or unsupported, or when life is getting the better of you?'

Ruth thought about this for a minute. 'Yes, now that you mention it.'

I explained that her grandmother had had a tough life and had decided to be Ruth's guardian to watch over her during challenging periods because she wanted to give her all the love and support she needed.

Ruth was happy to finally have answers about the presence in her house and even happier to discover it was her grandmother's spirit.

Sensitive kids can pick up lots of activity in houses. Tristan takes it in his stride. Others are learning to as well, because these children are here to work with higher consciousness and a new reality. Part of that reality is to understand alternative states of awareness and to work with Spirit. Tristan didn't have to shoo this spirit away, he eagerly picked up on its true nature. There is a difference between a spirit guide who is here to help you and a lost soul who, for the most part, is trying to find their way home. Your psychic child can tell the difference. Doesn't it give you peace of mind knowing how clued in they really are?

36
IT FELT RIGHT

Children don't always announce their good deeds to others in order to get a gold star. Maybe it's because they don't think they're doing anything special, or they are guided to do it, so what is there to say? They listen to their teacher's instructions in the classroom but that doesn't necessarily mean they come home and tell you everything they were told to do. And since spirit guides and the higher self act as teachers, kids don't think twice about following their guidance. Whether they are listening to what Spirit tells them, or whether they are following the 'If it feels right, then do it' mantra, it can lead to some incredibly beautiful acts of random kindness.

It was during the parent and teacher interview at the end of the year that I became aware of Chiara's activities at school.

'And you must be so proud of her?' Ms Lye said as she closed Chiara's subject report file.

'Of course,' I said without thinking. I knew Chiara was one of the 'good kids' who were well-mannered and not disruptive in class.

The teacher must have sensed that I didn't quite get what she was implying and added, 'You know how she helps kids in kindergarten?'

'Oh, yeah, you mean with the buddy system?'

Chiara's school assigned the seniors in the primary school to act as a buddy for kids in the younger grades. They took on the role of mentors who acted as a 'big brother or sister' to show kids the ropes and help them out whenever they needed it. I knew Chiara had looked after a few kids from different classes.

Ms Lye raised an eyebrow. 'I'm talking about what your daughter has been doing before class, during recess and during lunchtime.'

'Chiara hasn't told me about anything in particular.'

Chiara's teacher explained that when Chiara arrived at school she regularly checked the playground for juniors who needed help. If she saw someone who was looking lost, she went over to them and offered to help. Then, during recess and lunch Chiara organised her friends to accompany her into the playground and around the canteen area. If a child was crying, or looking lonely, Chiara's group would befriend them and help them find new friends. If someone was hungry, Chiara organised food. Once she had taken care of everyone's needs, she and her friends would go off and play.

How did I miss that one? I knew Chiara was a good-hearted kid. When it comes to helping her friends, and counselling them, she's a natural. She's sixteen now and still doing it. As I mentioned earlier, Chiara's soul urge is to help others and she has definitely awakened to this desire.

'I'm surprised she hasn't said something to you,' Ms Lye said.

'All I know is that Chiara calls me from school because she's forgotten her lunch. But when I get there she asks me to buy drinks or food for her friends.'

'Didn't you notice the younger kids?'

'Yes, but Chiara likes to have friends of all ages. Are you saying that some of those kids only just met her?'

'Yes,' said the teacher. 'They were the kids she was helping out because their parents forgot to pack their lunch, or they dropped their food in the playground.'

'I can believe that, but I'm still surprised she never bothered to tell me.'

When I got home from the meeting I asked Chiara about it.

She shrugged her shoulders. 'It just felt like the right thing to do.'

'Is that because of what I've taught you or something the teachers have said?'

'Yeah, but it's more than that. Mum, sometimes when I'm standing near another kid I feel sad or I feel angry or hurt. I kind of *know* what they're feeling without them saying anything. And if I'm feeling like I can help, I ask them to tell me what's wrong.'

'You're going with what feels right? That's fantastic,' I said, realising that it was her soul urge prompting her. 'How long have you been doing this sort of stuff?'

She shook her head. 'I don't know, I've been doing it for as long as I can remember. It started when I heard a voice in my head telling me to help this kid in kindy. It was a little boy and he was standing alone outside the toilets. The voice told me to talk to him.'

'And what was wrong with him?' I asked.

'He had no friends. His dad was in the army and they had just moved here. He didn't like being on his own all the time.'

'What did you do to help him?'

'I told him to come with me. I grabbed my handball and we played. Then the next day I did the same thing. Then this other kindy boy came over and asked if he could play with us too. I sort of got them to be friends,' she said, smiling.

Adults aren't the only ones to practise random acts of kindness. Children do it too. Most random acts of kindness happen in the spur of the moment. Something tweaks inside you and a *sense* or a *feeling* comes over you, propelling you to go out of your way to help. You don't stop and rationalise what you are doing. You just do it because it feels like the right thing to do. Your inner self has guided you to help make a difference to someone in need, even a total stranger. Your simple act can create a pocketful of miracles for others.

37

COMING TO YOUR SENSES

Having a psychic child is a blessing because it can help awaken your own intuitive abilities, just like Liz discovered. She realised that her kids were experiencing some extraordinary things and she didn't want to be left out of the picture. Liz recognised the importance of identifying and nurturing her own children's psychic reality and felt it was time to develop her own skills.

'Why don't I have your skills, Sue?' she asked when I turned up to do a psychic reading for her. 'If I can experience for myself what my kids see and if I can talk about it, then things will be easier.' She paused momentarily then added, 'It's okay, I know that one day I will be working with my own psychic ability.'

We talked for a short while then she announced that she would like to study metaphysics with me, which is a psychic, spiritual and personal development course, in order to understand the processes her children were going through and gain enough knowledge to be their rock.

'To have Richard as a psychic is actually comforting to me,' she told me over a cup of tea after I did a psychic reading for her. 'But, you know, I have to constantly validate him,' she stressed, understanding his need for support.

'Richard didn't start talking until he was two and a half years old. But by the time he was three, he was coming out with statements like, "Before, when I was big . . ." referring to past lives. Even now he comes to me and says things like, "Mum, I had this vivid dream where I've been here before."'

The momentum picked up over the years, then one night Richard came out of his room and said, 'I can't sleep, there's too many people in my room.' Liz advised him to tell his ethereal visitors, 'I need to sleep, go for now.'

Throughout these kinds of experiences she was sensitive enough to continue supporting his reality. She purchased a dream-catcher and placed it above the bedhead, assuring him that it would help him have good dreams and protect him. She placed an amethyst crystal under his bed to facilitate protection. He surprised her by moving it to the doorway, saying, 'This is where it needs to go.' Liz also put salt under his bed to absorb negative energy to make him feel more comfortable in his room.

To help Richard exercise his intuition, she filled a bowl with small, polished crystal pebbles. 'He could choose which crystal to take to bed that day, and which one to take to school. It was a power thing,' Liz explained. 'Richard called them his "power rocks" and it made him feel much better carrying one in his pocket.'

Interestingly, Richard often chose a tiger's eye, which is said to boost confidence. And Liz believes it made a difference, especially when he had to stand up in front of the class. Richard hated public speaking, but putting his hand into his pocket and rubbing the tiger's eye gave him a sense of calm, boosting his confidence in front of other kids.

Then something happened that was destined to really facilitate Richard and his sisters' psychic abilities. Their father Gordon was stricken with an incurable cancer. Gordon wasn't even forty years old. He was a fun, loving and easy-going dad.

During this difficult period, Liz decided to make up cards with pictures of archangels to help Richard. Liz would encourage him to select an archangel card daily and he would place it in his pencil case to help him feel protected and connected during this time of upheaval. Richard especially loved the archangels Metatron and Michael and still has a picture of Archangel Metatron on his bedroom wall. She also bought positive-affirmation cards for children. 'Richard and his sisters Emily and Maddie would shuffle the deck and select a card for the day before going off to school. It helped them to gain clarity or to focus on a specific strength,' she said.

Gordon was ill for four years. One day Richard told his father to hold a crystal 'because it might help you get better.' Unfortunately, despite all of Gordon's efforts to beat the disease, it became clear that he was going to die. Richard's intuition kicked in and told him not to 'pray for Daddy to survive, but for him to cross over safely and be with loved ones and to be totally pain free.'

Towards the end Gordon was in a palliative care hospital. During those five days Liz stayed with him while the kids visited as often as they wanted to. She was careful to give each of them private time with their father as well as time together as a family.

He wasn't conscious, but they all spoke to him and thanked him for their time together.

Liz started relying on her own intuition more and more, even though she didn't realise that she was opening up to her psychic abilities. She could feel the energy in Gordon's room. 'It felt warm and safe, which helped the kids cope,' she said.

The afternoon before Gordon died, Richard said, 'I'm not coming back, I've said enough goodbyes, he's going to be okay.' Richard is a highly sensitive child who, at thirteen, was dealing with having to close a painful chapter in his life and his inner knowing told him what to do. He later told me, 'While I am really sad, I didn't want to be selfish. I didn't want him to be in pain anymore. I knew that by letting him go it would mean that he was free.' Richard understood this and made his peace and didn't feel the need to be in the room anymore.

Richard's sisters Emily and Madeline left at 10.30 that night, just hours before Gordon died. 'We gave him a hundred kisses on the brow, to give him our permission for him to go,' Liz said. 'Even though he was unconscious, I knew his soul knew exactly what I was saying, what the kids had said earlier . . . he knew.

'I told Gordon, "I am proud of you, thank you for being a great father and husband, and providing us with a happy life." When he died it was amazing. I felt a kiss on my own forehead, then moments later he took his last breath.'

Liz is a lot more psychic than she realises. Gordon's passing has been a trigger for her to come to her psychic senses. She is learning to develop them and to rely on them to keep up with her psychic kids but also to help her gain a deeper awareness of her own soul.

38
LOVE NEVER DIES

Coping with any kind of loss is difficult for kids but your psychic child has the ability to see things differently. They can draw on their empathy and compassion, and their innate higher consciousness, to grasp how there is a reality beyond the physical, and to help them heal through understanding. It certainly helps to have a loving and switched-on mother like Liz to smooth out the bumpy road.

Liz is a remarkably strong woman. As she opened up more and gave me intimate details on how the family worked together to help prepare for Gordon's funeral, I could see the depth of her inner strength.

One of the things that helped her deal with Gordon's pending death was the recent death of his cousin Jenny.

'Jenny's passing helped me and the kids prepare for when Gordie went. It also gave Gordon a safe place to let go of his own pain, anguish and fear of his own death. Since Jenny's funeral was such a beautiful funeral it hit a deep chord within us,' Liz revealed. 'We were always conscious of trying to be positive before the funeral for Gordon's sake, but Jenny's funeral allowed us all to cry. It was cathartic.'

Attending Jenny's funeral prompted Gordon to make his own slide show. 'We chose the readings and songs together. He even chose the flowers. It was kind of surreal but it had to be done and the whole process made it easier for the kids because their dad had taken part in the arrangements, validating that he was okay with the journey back to the spirit world,' she said, her voice full of admiration.

Liz then continued to help the kids stay connected with their father. 'I left the door open,' she said. 'We went away to the south coast immediately after the funeral so we could talk about things, like if they felt his presence, if there were any messages coming through in their dreams, how they felt about everything.' It is this kind of support that gave the kids a clear message; it is okay to use their psychic gifts to keep the link with their father. Just because he is in spirit doesn't mean he has stopped caring about them. 'We make a point of talking to him every day, keeping that bond with his spirit alive.'

Since Gordon's passing he has definitely stayed connected with his family.

Liz told me, 'We had an incident when the lightbulb exploded when we were talking about him, and the kids said, "It's Dad . . . Good one, Dad!" Ever since then every time the family sits outside in the courtyard, the outdoor fan turns itself on and they know it is Gordon.

Liz revealed that Gordon is very much alive to her in spirit. 'He flicks on my bedside lamp at 10.30 every night. This is a significant time because it was the time when the girls last saw him. It's another spirit calling card from him, saying, "Good night, sleep tight."'

Richard smiled as he recalled, 'One day we were looking at photos of Dad and talking about his parents. Suddenly some of his photos went flying to the floor, face up. It was really funny. We were laughing so much. We knew it was Dad. We knew there was nothing to be scared of. His message was, "Stop talking about my parents, I can hear everything that you're saying."'

It was lovely to see the family maintaining a great sense of humour because it helps them deal with the reality of their loss.

Everywhere they look they see constant reminders of Gordon. 'We saw butterflies every day for a month after he died, rainbows and white feathers, which were our personal signs that he was around us,' Liz said. 'We don't feel overly sad because we feel we have an active connection with him. Even though we still miss him deeply, it's not from despair or fear, it comes from a loving space. I think preparation was the key. Gordon had a strong belief in the afterlife which helped him accept his death and his journey, but it also helped the kids come to terms with it.'

Liz recalled holding Gordon's hand and saying, 'When you die, I'm going to see a clairvoyant and if you don't come through I'll kill you!' As it turns out she did visit a clairvoyant and as soon she walked in the psychic said, 'Oh, Gordie died.' Then she added, 'Don't worry, you don't have to kill him!'

Liz burst into tears. 'I got my validation that his spirit was alive and well.' She knew that she and the kids wouldn't have to worry about him anymore.

After that Liz went home and told the kids they were going to pack up their father's stuff. 'Richard and I did the packing and then the girls came in. They all chose one jumper each to keep, and Richard kept his watch, ring and other personal things, but his clothes went to an autistic men's home. We could feel Gordie watching, it felt right, we just intuitively knew that it was the right time, even though we were criticised by others who thought it was too early.'

Liz chose to renovate the house, a symbol of the family's new beginning. 'Yes, we have photos of him in every room but we had to start a new chapter. The whole process was very healing. It was healing for the four of us to choose what to do, what to change, to make decisions about the new kitchen . . . It was a detox feeling.'

Liz and the kids have suffered a great loss with Gordon passing away but they are a courageous and remarkable family. Not only are they learning how to heal themselves and move on with life, they are all keeping 'open' to his spirit. They sense when he is around, they talk with him and listen to what he has to say.

'A lot of our friends think that we are all nuts, but we know that what we sense psychically is true, we have had so many signs, or should I say gifts, that he is still looking after us.'

Liz gave packs of angel cards to the kids to use when they didn't want to talk about any concerns regarding the loss of their father or other issues. This simple tool gets them engaged with Spirit and lets angels step in and do the talking through the symbolic pictures and messages on the cards. Emily has the goddess cards, Richard uses Archangel Michael's cards for messages and Maddie uses angel cards. Uplifting and insightful, the cards give Emily, Maddie and Richard encouragement and help them find their strengths to deal with whatever they need to deal with.

The kids were also coping with a lot of external judgement; they felt like they were living in fishbowl, because other family members expected them to do things differently.

'People avoided us,' Liz said. 'They made broad statements like, "Oh my god, you are so strong," like it was a bad thing that we were not in pieces. They believed that in order to mourn, the kids and I should be in foetal positions despairing and waiting for others to repair us. But our strong spiritual belief and our intuition has made the whole journey a peaceful and meaningful one. We decided that if we have to find ourselves in this situation then we had better learn from it, not run and hide.'

There are many ways to use your psychic ability to communicate with family in spirit. Liz's kids rely on their sixth sense to keep that link open. But they also do lots of physical things to keep their connection with their father alive and well. Each of the kids has a special photo of themselves with their father, with a little angel next to the photo frame, so they have him there and can see him all the time. As well as the photos throughout the house, they have made stickers with beautiful messages to him to put on the walls. Emily and her boyfriend built a water fountain at the front of the house in his memory. The girls also express their connection with their father through poetry on Facebook.

Liz and the kids are doing what works for them. This is a special family who have turned adversity around to form a strong and loving relationship with their loved one on the other side.

It's never too late to start talking to your loved ones in spirit.

39
MAKE A WISH

Losing a loved one forever is hard to deal with because a part of our personal history has gone. When this happens many of us make a wish to have them back in our lives. Richard made that wish. He wanted to have his father in his life.

While I was talking with Liz after her psychic reading, Richard came home from school with scooter in hand and a grazed knee, which his mother attended to. Richard, who was still only thirteen, then sat down with hot chocolate and biscuits and joined our chat.

'I understand that you see things,' I began. 'That you see your dad?'

'Yes,' he said in a soft voice. 'At first I just saw shadows in the room.'

'Did you know what they were?'

'No, I didn't understand. I thought I was just seeing things. Then Mum went to a psychic lady after Dad died and this lady actually said that Dad had been visiting and to say hello. I hadn't told Mum about the shadows. After that I started to really see him.'

'How does he appear to you now?' I asked, eager to hear his response. Some kids see loved ones in spirit as light, others as translucent apparitions.

'He's got a white glow and wears a white suit. He said he would prefer a black suit but he is not allowed.' Both Richard and his mother laughed. 'The first time I saw him like that it was kind of a good feeling because I knew he was with me. Now he walks with me to school.'

'That's fantastic,' I said.

Richard nodded his head in agreement. 'He tells me things like, "Richard, you should pay more attention in class and stop talking." And when I have physical ed class, Dad changes into sports clothes and joins me. Having him walk to school with me makes me feel safe and happy. It also makes me miss him more, but I feel lucky too.' Tears began to well in Richard's eyes. 'So no matter what happens at school, I know I can talk to him and tell him how I feel. If I have a bad day at school, if I get bullied or something, he gives me advice, like "Tell those bullies to leave you alone".'

Richard also sees other spirits but doesn't know who they are. They are a mix of young and old. 'Sometimes Dad comes with a really short woman,' he added.

Liz immediately piped up, 'That's your great-grandmother. She's in heaven with him!' While I was doing the psychic reading for Liz, I tuned in and saw that Gordon was with his grandmother. I got an image of an extremely short woman and passed on several other details. This gave Liz further validation that Richard was really seeing his father.

We talked about heaven—it's a term most kids relate to—though I prefer to call it the spirit world or the astral plane. I asked Richard if he knew what his father was doing in heaven.

'Dad said the best bit about being in heaven is he can have whatever he wants. He just has to open up the fridge and there's food—custard and cake, his favourites! And there are no bills.'

Liz laughed. 'That's something Gordon would say, he was always grumbling about bills!'

'He says he's happy because there is no fighting but that bit kind of bores him.'

'Does he have any jobs there?' I asked.

'No, not jobs like here. But his "walk in the park" is to come to earth and to visit me when I walk to school. He can even bring his dog Rusty with him. On weekends he visits and sits by my bed at night but not on school nights when I'm doing homework. It's funny; sometimes Dad has to go back to heaven early and stuff, like he has a curfew.'

I explained that people who have recently died are still debriefing from this life. They are in a healing space and still assimilating to their new life in spirit. Obviously, when Gordon opens the fridge and grabs custard and cake he isn't eating physical food, but the memories and taste sensations are real. I pointed out to Richard that heaven was a new world for his father and he was still learning the ropes.

Imagine growing up in the Kalahari Desert and being sent to a large city without any preparation for what was going to happen to you. It would be a shock. Well, it's the same for people who have passed over. They need time to acclimatise to their new environment and be healed before they move on to the next stage of their journey. Even though Gordon is playing 'spirit guide' for

Richard, he is still in a transit phase in the spirit world and on a learning curve. Later on he will be able to see higher planes of existence.

'Dad tells me he is just like a teenager again; he has to learn new things. When I said, "But now you don't have to wear those old eighties clothes," he laughed and said, "Shut up," with a big smile.'

Liz commented that the family had been looking at pictures of Gordon when he was a teenager during the eighties, and how they had laughed at his clothes. 'So the joke is not lost on him. He knows we've been talking about him.'

Richard added, 'And the other thing I joke about is, "Wow, Dad, you still have a full head of hair!"'

Liz explained that Gordon's hairline had started receding when he was twenty-four.

'Dad changes how he looks, so one day he's got a mullet, and the next it's a completely different hairdo,' Richard said. 'It's kind of cool that he still has a great sense of humour.'

Richard then revealed, 'Before he died I thought heaven would be full of big fluffy white clouds with angels playing boring games with each other. Now I know that there is a lot more to heaven.

'Dad tells me heaven is just like down here, except that we're not there with him. He has the same house but it has a massive doorway. The front door opens up to his "heaven" and it's a happy place. A few times when he was still alive we went to Nan's house on the south coast but Dad had to stay home and work. So being in heaven is like that, his work keeps him in a different place to us for now.'

Richard got his wish—his father is still a very real part of his life.

During our conversation, Richard also told me that he knew his father's spirit visits his grandparents too.

'Dad says that he wants to check and make sure they're okay. Just before Mother's Day, he gave me a message: he said his brother Keith had hurt his leg badly. Later when I called Nanna to wish her a happy Mother's Day, she told me that Uncle Keith had injured his leg. Nanna doesn't believe in this kind of stuff so I didn't tell her. But I knew Mum would listen and she was really excited.'

Suddenly Richard's mood changed and his face clouded. 'But the other day Dad said he wouldn't be around to visit me so often for a while, because he would have to stay at Nanna and Pop's, 'cos Pop was going to get sick and would need him.'

A few days later Liz found out that Gordon's father had prostate cancer.

A lot of kids would love to have the same strong connection with their loved ones in spirit. When I mentioned this to Richard, he acknowledged, 'Yes, it makes me feel like I'm different to everyone else. Sometimes it makes me feel bad because other people don't understand. I've only told one of my friends. He said, "Yeah, okay," but I don't think he believed me. And the others would only laugh or make jokes about me if I told them.'

I explained that a lot of kids are in the same boat; they are aware but won't talk about it because they don't want others to laugh at them.

Liz added, 'My sister's eldest daughter Georgia, who is six years old, has also seen Gordon in the schoolyard but got frightened because she didn't understand why she could see him.'

Richard, like many psychic kids, is coming to terms with his abilities. He is happy that his psychic senses are keeping him close to his father and that the messages he receives are real. Gordon has passed on a number of messages, such as his father's illness and how his brother hurt his leg, before the family disclosed this information to Richard. Having his reality validated by evidence gives Richard the momentum to keep his psychic channel open. And it has taught him that his father's love is something special.

Gordon may not have a physical body but his essence, his soul, is around his family. His love and guidance help them to get on with life with a sense of security that comes from knowing that there is life after death.

We get so caught up in the hectic pace of living that we forget that loved ones in spirit are still a part of our lives. Their love is as real as it ever was. And psychic kids like Richard know this to be true.

40
INDIGO CHILDREN

Kids like Richard are indigo children. They are also part of Gen Y, kids born in the 1980s and 1990s, who are also called the 'Peter Pan' or 'Me' generation. We've all heard the generalisations about Gen Y—their lack of responsibility, their self-absorption, their dislike for authority, and they live in rapidly changing times of exploding technology and economic disruption. But there's more to Gen Y than meets the eye. They are also spiritually different.

The term 'indigo children' was coined by Nancy Anne Trappe who, while working at the University of San Diego, noticed a distinct change in the colour of aura of kids who were born in the eighties and nineties. She published a book on her research called *Understanding Your Life Through Color* (Aquila Libris Publishing, 1982). Tappe felt that the colour indigo suggested the type of life mission this generation of children would undertake.

Colours emanating from your aura reveal what is going on inside you at a physical, emotional, psychological and spiritual level—or the mind–body–soul connection. The amount and intensity of a particular colour in an aura will help you pinpoint exactly what someone is thinking, feeling or processing. For example, someone with lots of yellow in their aura is in their head a lot; someone with pink close to the physical body needs some TLC.

Colour changes in the aura are a fantastic indicator of what is going on inside your child's inner world. Your aura is your soul and other people feel and react to your soul's energy, even though you might not realise this. When you talk about someone's 'vibe' this is really what you are referring to. Your aura also has another colour overlay. It's a colour that defines your soul's purpose. Different generations have different takes on life, how they see and react to the world, and this is reflected in the overall colour of the aura. Indigo is the colour of the third-eye chakra, which is located in the centre of your forehead. The third-eye chakra governs your vision and perception of things, and regulates your clairvoyant abilities. Therefore, indigo children are seen as being very psychic because of the presence of this ray of indigo light in their auras. They also have a warrior spirit.

Tristan and Chiara are typical indigo children who are psychic and sensitive. Tristan used to get overwhelmed when he was young because he could literally *feel* and *know* what other kids were feeling and processing. Eventually, we taught him how to protect his energy so he wasn't being bombarded by other people's stuff. The upside of being psychic is that you can pick up even the most subtle energies; the downside is that you pick up too much of what's not yours. Being so young, Tristan didn't have a system in place that energetically separated *what was theirs* from *what was his*, so he often arrived home feeling scattered and emotionally confused. We taught him how to protect himself by creating a lovely golden cocoon of energy combined with the statement to 'Stay open to others but not absorb their stuff'.

Occasionally, his guard dropped and he absorbed others' feelings but this usually happened when he was being sympathetic or compassionate towards them. This problem was easily resolved when we taught him how to flush his aura (soul) with a beautiful pinkish white light and the statement, 'I let go of anything that is not mine'. He loved doing this simple exercise because it gave him instant results. Knowing that he could draw on a few psychic tools to handle the situation empowered him because he knew he could regulate what was going on within his own energy field. I feel this is such an important point—kids flourish psychically when they understand how it works.

He started questioning his reality because he could see auras and spirits walking through the classroom.

'How do I put the puzzle of my experiences together?' he asked me when he was sixteen. 'I'm waking up at night and seeing spirit guides by the foot of my bed!'

Like other psychic kids he was trying to figure out why this was happening to him.

'And there were also other beings who were watching over me,' he said.

'What kind of beings?' I asked.

'Really large whitish beings with a halo of strong colours around them, but I knew that they weren't spirit guides. They were evaluating me and telling me things like, "You are here to protect others".'

Thankfully Tristan found a sense of solidarity from watching an anime cartoon called *Dragon Ball* Z. The *Dragon Ball* Z characters used to send energy through them to fight the bad guys and protect the earth. This prompted Tristan to ask more about chakras, auras and energy to gain a better understanding of what he was experiencing. It made him feel better about his take on life because there were cartoon characters talking about the same things.

His 'crazy dreams'—his term for lucid dreaming, a dream where you are aware that you are actually dreaming—were often quite psychic. He also revealed, 'Sometimes, if I woke up from a bad dream and I didn't want to accept what had happened because it didn't feel right, I would go back to sleep and go to the same spot where I left off and change it, especially if I needed to be a warrior.'

Those familiar with my book *Sixth Sense* will recall how Tristan saw spirits sending bands of green light and telling him how he could use this energy to heal others. He could also see other dimensional realities.

Tristan has since agreed to help heal and protect others, a message Spirit has been giving him for years and is still telling him today. He told me, 'I believe this agreement is with very strong and high-up spiritual forces. They're not like any ghost or spirit guide I've ever seen.'

Recently, after the Fukushima disaster, two spirit guides appeared and instructed him on how to help send absentee healing energy for people in Japan. Like a true indigo warrior he is now working with what he calls 'dragon energy' to protect and heal others.

41
SUPER PSYCHICS

That's the upside of being an indigo child. These kids are psychic, sensitive and have a warrior spirit. But the strengths of the indigo soul are not always apparent because many of these children's abilities lie dormant, or they may be expressing the absolute polarity of the warrior nature, so it is in detriment. Even though indigos have the ability to work with both sides of the brain aligned, so their head and heart are unified and make it easier for them to access their intuitive intelligence, not all of them are taking advantage of this. Traditionally, in the West, we tend to favour left-brain thinking, which is analytical and logical, over the intuitive and creative right brain. Indigo children are trying to break that mould but it is hard when socially and culturally the focus is on the left brain.

If the warrior nature of indigos is not given the platform to be expressed properly, it can become rebellious, aggressive or hyperactive. Many indigo kids have been diagnosed as having ADHD and ADD. Sadly, I believe, the system has failed to recognise that indigo children have a higher vibration and soul purpose. So, instead of catering to their 'intensity' and rebelliousness, and tackling the problem from a spiritual perspective, many have been treated with mind-numbing drugs like Ritalin.

A practical solution would be to adapt education to suit the needs of these evolving souls instead of pumping them with medication. They are old souls packaged in young bodies; they have a different level of consciousness. We need to use a different yardstick to measure them by, not relying on old models of what we expect them to conform to. The truth is these kids are meant to be different. It is part of their soul journey to venture into new ground, to break down the old order and bring in fresh ideas and innovative ways of doing things. Because the third-eye chakra is the vision chakra, the indigo children are here to use abilities such as clairvoyance and telepathy to show us a different way of living. It is important that these children's talents are cultivated instead of being treated like a square peg that has to be pushed into a round hole.

It is interesting to hear how much the Chinese government values and encourages these kids, the 'super psychics'. In the book *China's Super Psychics* (Marlowe & Company, 1997), authors Paul Dong and Thomas E. Raffill reveal that the Chinese government has invested millions of dollars in researching what they call EHF, which stands for 'extra human function', in psychic kids. Back in 1997 it was estimated that more than 100 000 'super psychics' have been identified. The authors cite that Xiao Kiong, from Shanghai, was the first child under the program to be identified as having special gifts. She was tested for automatic writing, which is also known as psychic writing. In the test she was asked to visualise a few words written on paper that was folded and placed inside a pencil case. After the test the pencil case was opened and written on the paper were the exact words she visualised.

In another experiment in the Yunnan Province, five blindfolded psychic kids were asked to intuitively read what was on a page torn from a randomly selected book. The page was rolled into a ball and placed under the child's armpit and the child was asked to read every word on it. Remarkably, they did it!

This is just the tip of the iceberg. As these children, some of whom have already reached adulthood, continue to develop they will unmask some truly awesome abilities that will redefine how we see life. There is no limit to how far they can go. Subsequent generations, like the crystal, star and rainbow kids, will take this legacy and run with it, further developing the scope of human potential.

What I feel is important to stress here is that we have only had a glimpse of what people are capable of. In fifty years we will look back at the late twentieth century and the early twenty-first century and think to ourselves, 'Wow, couldn't they see what we see? Why didn't it click in for them when everything we know was right under their noses!'

At the beginning of the twentieth century the idea of landing on the moon was pure fantasy. Now we have google universe! The paranormal stayed in the domain of the occult, or the hidden, explored by only a small section of the community. Over the years technology has radically transformed. Quantum science now talks about different dimensional realities and parallel universes, and kids are growing up watching cartoons and movies that make terms like meditation and chakra and the paranormal part of everyday life. There is so much more we can do with our psychic ability. It is a work of art in progress.

In the future working openly with psychic abilities will be part of everyday life and no one will question it. Your gifted child is paving the way for us to forge ahead into a new way of living—a holistic, intuitive and connected way.

42

THE PSYCHIC GENERATION

It's all about change. The new kids on the block are different and we should celebrate and honour their uniqueness and exercise acceptance and tolerance. We need to help them feel great about being themselves. If we don't, then some may end up feeling like misfits or experience difficult relationships.

There's no denying nine-year-old Ruby is telepathic. In the schoolyard, standing at a distance from a group of friends, she tunes in and knows exactly what they are talking about. Their voices aren't carried on the wind; she can't physically hear them. Instead she telepathically picks up on their intimate conversations. When she approaches them and reveals what she knows, they are astounded.

Even her mother and grandmother are surprised by her ability. Ruby can walk into the house after school and repeat verbatim a conversation between them and she is 100 per cent right.

Does your child sometimes read your mind? Have you noticed the signs of telepathic ability in your child or perhaps in other kids you know? Signs like picking up on feelings and then telling you exactly what you're thinking about. Or when they come out with incredible statements like, 'No, you shouldn't buy the red car,' when you've just come back from a car sales yard without telling them where you've been. Or when they look you straight in the eye and before you've finished a sentence, they've done it for you and it could be on a subject that they know nothing about.

It's an ability that seems to be raging like a bushfire across the globe. More and more kids are displaying telepathy. The new kids on the block are incredible little souls—and they can be truly gifted psychics. Called the 'crystal children' because of the opalescent sheen in their aura, they are children born after 2000. Known for their fascination with crystals, this generation of kids displays remarkable telepathic skills. Astute parents will have already noticed this ability in their child. Others are slowly discovering that there is 'something different' about them even though they can't put their finger on what it is.

Rainbow children are souls who have never before incarnated on earth. Also born from 2000 onwards, they are instilled with unity consciousness, so they are destined to bring harmony and joy to others. They have forgiving hearts and are here to give—that is their spiritual gift. They are sometimes referred to as the star children. Star children is a term that is used to describe a grouping of souls which includes indigo, crystal and rainbow kids.

Prominent metaphysician Doreen Virtue agrees that today's kids are very telepathic and believes that these children may delay speech. Why? To force parents to use other means of communication, namely telepathy. It's an interesting perspective. In a world of lightning-fast telecommunications via the internet and mobile phones, the old way of thinking and doing things has changed forever. We live in an information-overloaded society, one where we expect information at the click of a finger. And while this kind of technology is fantastic for business or for kids doing assignments or interacting with friends, I feel that it's a precursor to something profoundly significant to do with our soul evolution. It signals the beginning of new ways of working with our senses.

As you know, technology changes in the blink of an eye and the only way to keep up with the pace is to adapt to the changing parameters. This means our brains have to be used differently. We have to change our perception of the world, and how we deal with it. Children are being born with the right mix of innovation and intuition to help keep up with technology. Unlike a lot of people who are aged in their seventies and beyond who find it difficult to adapt to new technologies because they grew up in such a different world, the crystal children are born into this environment. They're hardwired to keep up with the changes. Being telepathic means they are working with a different way of accessing and sending information, so they are effectively keeping one step ahead of the game.

Ruby doesn't quite understand her telepathic abilities as well as some of the other things she is experiencing. It drives her mad sometimes. One day she accused her mother of pulling the back of her hair.

'I didn't pull your hair. Perhaps it was one of your playmates?' her mother told her, referring to her imaginary friends.

'My head still hurts. This is real.'

'I didn't touch you.'

Ruby doesn't know what to believe. This kind of thing keeps happening. Is she going crazy?

'Things got out of hand,' said Marie, a close family friend. 'Pent-up frustration got the better of Ruby and she started throwing things around the room. Poor kid doesn't know what else to do. Her mother doesn't know how to handle it so she's sent her to stay with her father. Now she only sees her every second weekend.'

Marie added that Ruby is a beautiful kid, very rowdy and strong-willed. This is why her mother doesn't know if what Ruby is doing is a performance or real.

'What does she think is wrong with Ruby?' I asked Marie.

'She's not sure. She worries that Ruby's got a mental health issue. But if it is something like that, then it's sad because she doesn't know how to explain it or approach the problem.'

This is what parents worry about: 'Is my child delusional or can they really see and feel things I can't?'

Marie asked me to visit Ruby and see if I can help. She told me Ruby is very, very clever but Marie is worried that if someone doesn't put in a safety net Ruby may come undone.

Intuitive herself, Marie has approached Ruby a few times and asked her to talk about what's been happening. The last time they spoke Ruby opened up and said, 'Can you see the white lady with the ginger cat around her?'

'When do you see her?' Marie asked.

'All of the time, she follows me.'

'Are you talking about your ginger cat?'

'Yes,' replied Ruby. 'The white lady is always around her.'

'Maybe you are seeing things through your cat's eyes?' suggested Marie. 'Did you know that some kids are telepathic? It means you can see what is going on in someone else's mind. Perhaps you can see what is going through the cat's mind?'

It was food for thought; Marie gave a lifeline to Ruby. It was refreshing for her to hear an adult encourage an open discussion on what she was sensing.

I am keen to meet Ruby. Hopefully I can help her, and help her mother to understand and resolve their problems. Children like Ruby have so many talents and they can open our eyes to so many things. They just need the right level of support.

43

CRYSTAL CLEAR

No doubt it's disheartening for parents of those crystal children who also happen to have conditions like autism and ADHD to have others think their kids are dysfunctional. What about their unique gifts? Another thing that is often overlooked is the spiritual cause behind their different ways of expressing themselves. I know these conditions are on the rise and, yes, the environment and genetics do have an influence, but these conditions can be seen to go hand in hand with spiritual evolution as well. If you look at the bigger picture, there is a reason why these children are born with disabilities. Spirit is trying to teach us to open up to and embrace new ways of communicating and relating, and these children help us to see that.

Autistic kids are highly sensitive to energy, yet to the outer world they appear withdrawn and disconnected. Perhaps it is our own labelling system, or the way we classify what is normal, that is at fault and needs to be revised. Certainly there is an argument for the suggestion that environmental causes such as chemicals and pollution are responsible for the increase in autism and ADHD. But on a spiritual level I believe that we all choose our parents as well as their culture and environment. The incarnating soul is fully aware of the environment it has selected to be born into and understands the limitations and karmic lessons associated with being born with a condition like autism.

I'm going out on a limb here but this is what I feel is going on in the periphery. These kids are actually more connected than we think. They simply connect differently because they are caught between two realities. They live in the physical world with a physical body and physical lessons to learn. But they are also highly sensitive and can sense and feel many different frequencies of energy. In fact, the problem often stems from sensory overload, which is why they withdraw. Imagine having the incredible ability to tune into other realms of reality simultaneously. What if you could connect with the energetic world of Spirit while trying to live in the physical world? You'd have information flooding you from all directions, yet as a young child and you wouldn't understand how to manage this onslaught of information.

A relative of mine has Asperger's syndrome, a form of autism. He scored the most incredible grades at school so no one pegged him as autistic. Although intelligent, he recognised a tendency towards emotionally inappropriate behaviour. He realised he lacked empathy. It worried him and as a result he researched his symptoms on the internet when he was sixteen. After he told his parents about his concerns, they took him for an evaluation and the psychiatrist confirmed his condition.

The autistic savant is another type of autism. They are geniuses.

What they lack emotionally or socially is more than compensated for with a specific brilliance. Some of you will remember Dustin Hoffman's character in the movie *Rain Man* who was an autistic savant and mathematical genius. Daniel Tammet is also a mathematical genius. His ability to calculate the most complex maths is astounding.

But the most intriguing thing about Daniel is that he does not consciously make the calculations. Answers come instantly, naturally. And he sees numbers in a unique visual way. 'The number two, for instance, is a motion, and five is a clap of thunder. "When I multiply numbers together, I see two shapes. The image starts to change and evolve, and a third shape emerges. That's the answer. It's mental imagery. It's like maths without having to think."'[2]

As a kid Daniel was teased for being different; other kids didn't understand why he would go into the playground at school, but not play. Daniel explained, 'The place was surrounded by trees. While the other children were playing football, I would just stand and count the leaves.'[3]

This gives us a rare insight into the world of the autistic child, information that many cannot share or explain. While a lot of autistic people can't express why things happen, Daniel can, and his information is helping scientists to better understand the nature of autism.

Brain scans suggest autistic savants use their right brain. This fits in with my belief that they are using a higher level of intuitive intelligence because the right side of the brain is the intuitive, creative part of the brain. Also, because their transpersonal point, which is situated at the top of the aura, is wide open, they experience sensory overload. The transpersonal point isn't a chakra, but an energy centre, so it doesn't hold a seat of consciousness. It's really a centre that your soul uses to regulate exactly how much information is allowed to come into your mind at any one time. Autistic children don't have the same energetic filters as other people, so they don't have a system in place that blocks out information overload.

Daniel interprets information differently to most, but like other autistic people he gets information overload. He doesn't like going to supermarkets because 'there's too much mental stimulus'. He explained, 'I have to look at every shape and texture. Every price, and every arrangement of fruit and vegetables. So instead of thinking, "What cheese do I want this week?", I'm just really uncomfortable.'[4]

We could all benefit from rewiring how we see these incredible children. We need to acknowledge that each of us processes things differently, like Pattie, who is an inspiring example to all of us.

Jenny was a bright and bubbly single mother. She died recently from breast cancer, leaving behind her twelve-year-old autistic son Patrick. During the last precious months of her life, her parents moved in to help her and to ease the transition for Patrick into his grandparents' care. His grandmother, Pattie, has always had a close and loving relationship with Patrick, who also has an intellectual disability along with autism.

To cope with the loss of his mother, Patrick began a communication routine to help him keep the bond of love between him and Jenny's spirit.

Pattie told me that Patrick, without any prompting, started saying, 'Can I talk to Mummy's star in the sky?' Now he does it all the time. He will go out under the night sky and tell Jenny about his day. On nights when the stars are not too clear, he'll say, 'I want to talk to Mummy's moon.'

'What does he say to her?' I asked Pattie.

'He'll tell her about what he did during the day, or what he wants to do tomorrow. We do a lot of fun things when he is talking to his mother, we joke about things and make it light and bright.'

Patrick loves being under the stars, and talking makes him feel even closer to his mother.

'It is an intimate thing, it's hard for me to describe,' Pattie said. 'Sometimes, he will go out a second time, usually before bedtime, and say a quick hello again.'

Since Patrick has an intellectual disability, he does not express himself like other children. When he was little, Jenny taught him to express himself through visual means, such as telling a story by laying down picture cards. This has always worked for him. Yet people often underestimate his keen perception.

'He misses nothing,' Pattie said. 'His hearing is absolutely accurate.'

Children with disabilities often develop extra abilities to compensate for lacking another medium. In Patrick's case it is his hearing, and also his ability to pick up and read vibes.

Pattie emphasised this point. 'One day he was downstairs in the playroom when I was upstairs talking to a builder about renovations. The sound doesn't carry well and most people wouldn't hear anything but Patrick does. He came upstairs and asked, "Where are we going to live?"'

Patrick might not always express what he knows in words, but he is extremely aware of what is going on.

'He picks up on other people's feelings, and even when people talk over him thinking he doesn't understand, he does. He doesn't miss a beat,' Pattie said proudly.

I asked Pattie if he picks up when she is sad. 'Oh yes, every time, even though I'm often trying not to show it. And he knows I pick up on him. The other night I knew he was sad. He was in bed and I felt he wanted to cry and told him. The next thing he flung his arms around my neck and started sobbing. He misses his mother a lot but can't express it with visuals when he is in bed. So I tune in, pick up on what he is feeling and say it for him, and he can then let out his feelings through crying or hugging me.'

Patrick and Pattie have a very special bond and it's based on trust. 'Patrick trusts me implicitly. I never tell him a lie because he will know. He always knows when others are lying to him. They're silly; they stick him in the disabled category and fail to see his talents and how perceptive he is. Patrick feels their vibes. He always knows the phoneys.'

Disabled children like Patrick are very special young souls. They see the world differently and communicate information differently, but we should never underestimate their talents. They are intuitive and know a lot more than many people give them credit for. These beautiful souls are insightful and caring, and can and do play a special role in this world.

Imagine being able to create a healthy energetic boundary to help sensitive kids monitor what kind of information is coming in, so they can find a balance between these two worlds. I believe that future generations will have this down pat. These kids are the fringe-dwellers who are here to test-drive new ways of working with both the physical world and the spirit world at the same time. Subsequent generations will assimilate into the combined worlds so much more easily because of the groundwork now being laid down by the crystal kids. Don't forget they are here to break down the old world view many people are audaciously holding onto.

That world is crumbling and a new reality is emerging—one that will enable us all to connect with new worlds.

Although some crystal children have autism and ADHD, the majority don't. If you peel away the surface, you will see that crystal children are compassionate, caring and have wonderful psychic gifts, even the knack for healing. They are born with psychic abilities that will help them see things crystal clear.

We can learn a lot from these talented kids if we think beyond the box and embrace them for being exactly who they are.

44

SWITCHED ON

Luke has Down syndrome. A lot of people tend to discount him, overlooking his talents because they do not understand his condition. They label children with learning difficulties as being 'not smart enough to understand' or they might say something like, 'They don't have the capacity to read situations correctly'. Parents of intellectually disabled children know there is a lot more to their children, especially when it comes to their intuitive abilities.

When I walked into Sandra's home I was greeted by boisterous blond-haired, cheeky-grinned Luke. He raced up to me and grabbed my hand. 'Come,' he said determinedly. 'Let's draw.' I duly followed him into the kitchen where pencils, crayons and drawing books were spread over the table.

'Sit,' he commanded. 'Draw.'

Luke's elder brother Matthew, who was sitting in the family room watching television, looked up and caught my eye. 'You'd better draw,' he warned playfully.

'Draw,' repeated Luke, handing me a red pencil. I started colouring the picture in the colouring book. 'Later, we can watch TV,' he said, happily drawing away.

I was impressed by how refreshingly open Luke was, a real social butterfly and so eager to connect with me. He was effervescent, and his infectious smile and beautiful energy made me laugh.

His mother Sandra came out from the therapy room where she does remedial massage. Her client left and Sandra laughed at me. 'So, you've met Luke?'

'Yes.' I smiled back. 'We're drawing.'

'He likes your energy,' she said. 'A lot of the respite carers that come over here are very open and so Luke takes to them quickly. He can always spot an open person.'

'He is very intuitive, isn't he?' I said. Many people think that Down syndrome children tend to be guarded, so it's hard for them to see that they have intuition. These people interpret their cautious body language as a sign that the kid is unaware, when they are really switched on.

'Do you feel you are intuitive as well?' I asked Sandra. 'Does having Luke make you rely more on your instincts?'

'I think having children increases our intuition. I was telling a friend the other day how life is always unpredictable with Luke and how some people watch me interacting with him and say, "Oh, I don't know how you do it." They don't realise that life has prepared me for him,' she said.

There is an old saying that 'Special people have special kids' but Sandra doesn't particularly believe it; she feels she developed the skills to work with Luke's unpredictability because she grew up in an unpredictable household.

'I also tend to be able to read his next move, and therefore to me it's not unpredictable. It doesn't stress me out,' she explained. 'And I think, as far as my journey to develop my intuitive abilities and spiritual beliefs goes, Luke has made me more accepting of some of the old sayings like "Things are meant to be" and "Sometimes you've got to give your problems to a higher being" or "You can only control what you can". Having Luke in my life has made me think differently about things.'

Sandra believes that as a child she was very intuitive but it was pushed aside. But, as an adult, she learnt to call on her intuition constantly. 'Because at times there is nothing else to call on.'

Six years ago, when Luke was two, Sandra and her husband separated and since then she has to do everything on her own. Raising a child with Down syndrome without much family living close to support her presents a unique set of challenges for her. But her sixth sense has been a crux to fall back on.

'Since being on my own, what I have found myself doing more and more is really listening to that gut instinct that you get about things at times, without questioning it,' she revealed. 'When I was married I used to question my intuition all the time. I used to think logically and ended up doing the wrong thing. But since Luke was three I started relying on it more and more because there was no other option. It's a fantastic resource. Luke is getting more robust now, so relying on my intuition is a great support, but when he was little his health was very fragile and it used to change very quickly so I would have to make a judgement call on the spot and make the best of that decision. My gut instincts were always right.'

Like other parents of intellectually disabled children, Sandra knows that his communication can be unclear; he can't always specifically tell her what he wants.

'Luke can't always express what he wants with words so I have to anticipate and read him. Sure, I will use prompts like body and sign language, but often it is that inner knowing that helps me tune in and give him what he needs.'

Sandra's other son Matthew also relies on his psychic impressions, especially when communicating with his brother. Fourteen-year-old Matthew's sense of intuition is rapidly developing.

'Matthew is very sensitive in those things, so there's a strong psychic bond between them,' said Sandra. 'They have a little thing going; basically, Matthew is able to know, feel and sense exactly what Luke needs and wants without him saying. Matthew gives Luke a beautiful platform. From the time Luke was born, Matthew has always wanted to help and play with him. He is very protective of him. And Luke is equally protective of Matthew, funnily enough. They have always been wonderful together.'

I could see that Luke was very caring and Sandra confirmed this. 'He loves babies. He's always wanting to kiss and cuddle them. I think he just clicks with babies; he's drawn to them and very gentle with them. It's like he links into their energies. He's also very close to animals.' Sandra added that Luke also has a great sense of humour.

Another wonderful attribute he has is that Luke is a skilled problem-solver. Sandra said, 'If he needs something and he can't get the help, he will figure out how to solve the problem. He is very clever in that sense and I am sure that this has developed from his inability to be heard or understood by others.'

Because Luke is sometimes challenged to get the right word out, he'll stick to what feels right for him, which some people misinterpret as being 'stubborn'. There are a lot of generalisations out there, and labelling Down syndrome children as stubborn is one of them.

'Aren't we all?' Sandra stated. 'But instead of calling us stubborn, people say we're sticking to our guns so it's okay. When a child with Down syndrome sticks to theirs, they do it with less verbalisation, so people misread it as stubbornness. In fact, it's a protection thing. These kids are really trying to say, "I am uncomfortable, and if I could say it you would leave me alone."'

Sandra compares Luke's communication to the same problem new migrants have with their language skills. 'You have talented doctors and scientists doing menial labour here because of their poor command of English. People tag them as being simple because of the job they have at the moment, not realising that many of them have PhDs.'

She is right. A lot of people don't understand the world of people with Down syndrome. This is largely due to the fact that they aren't exposed to their world, so naturally they might not understand the ins and outs of what is in the heart of an intellectually delayed child. These children are able to pick up information through their psychic impressions. You might not see it from a distance, but when you get close to a Down syndrome child like Luke, their smile tells you all—they are very aware.

45
TRUSTING SOULS

Luke uses his psychic impressions to work out who he can trust. Kids who are trained to sit in their left brain will naturally lean towards logic to analyse something before trusting it. Children who favour the right side of the brain will *feel* what they can trust. Because Sandra is a single mum with no relatives living close by, she relies on respite carers for the much-needed occasional night out and down time from her immense responsibilities as the mother of two children, one with Down syndrome.

'We've had many different respite carers over the years and usually Luke is good with them,' Sandra said. 'But there was one lady who came over and I immediately got a bad feeling about her. Luke didn't take to her at all; he kept pushing her away and didn't want anything to do with her.' Both mother and son intuitively sensed the same thing. 'Even when I arrived home he was sitting on the floor with his back to the carer, he still wouldn't acknowledge her.'

Sandra trusts his intuition. She relies on it whenever a new respite carer arrives. 'Three weeks later we had a young fellow about twenty-two come over and I felt comfortable with him, he was wanting information about Luke, he was listening to me. Luke came and took him by the hand and said, "Come on, let's go do a puzzle."'

Luke trusts his psychic impressions; for him it is a survival thing because he hasn't developed the rational basis to assess people yet, but he knows he can rely on his intuition.

I asked Sandra if Luke intuitively picks up on her own thoughts and feelings.

'He picks up on my emotions a lot,' she revealed. 'I try to smile about things but he knows when something is wrong. He will come up and give me a hug and a kiss and pat me on the back. He'll smile at me and try to cheer me up, or he will call out, "Matthew, come," and get Matthew to give me a kiss and hug as well.'

I wondered if Luke's highly developed intuitive abilities gave him access to the spirit world.

'He senses Spirit; although he tends to be a bit of an actor, and he does at times act out scenes from movies, so it can be misleading,' Sandra admitted. 'However, I sense the difference between when he is acting and when he is honestly having a conversation with someone, particularly at bedtime.'

Luke will talk with spirits in front of his mother until she says, 'Come on, you need to go to sleep, say goodnight.' Then Luke will end the conversation with his ethereal visitors, wave goodbye to them and kiss his mother goodnight.

'I can feel the energies of the spirits myself,' Sandra added. 'At times I have said to the spirits, "You need to go, Luke needs to go to sleep."'

They are a psychic family. Matthew also feels the presence of Spirit. He feels temperature changes in a room. A spirit guide or family member in spirit can alter the temperature, often creating pockets of cold energy. Matthew feels the vibrational changes when spirits are around but he takes it in his stride. Knowing that an ethereal being is in the room does not disturb him.

Sandra said that sometimes, after she has given a client a remedial massage, Matthew will suddenly announce, 'I am just going to burn some sage.' Burning sage releases an uplifting essence which makes it harder for negative energies to hang around. Without any prompting from her, Matthew intuitively senses the need to cleanse their space of residual negativity.

Sandra is blessed with two very special, beautiful boys. They help keep her positive. She takes uncertainty and adversity in her stride. She had a tough childhood, and things are still tough, yet she remains optimistic no matter what life throws at her. Even though she is going through personal challenges at the moment, she manages to hold up better than most. She stated, without hesitation, 'My children are my motivation to get through the hardships in my life.'

Having spent an hour in the company of this close-knit family, feeling the energy of their open and loving souls, I was positively uplifted. Sandra, Luke and Matthew have a strong, mutual bond. They help each other because they *feel* and *know* what the other needs. It helps the household run smoothly, even when Luke is being boisterous and needs attention. It's a reminder that all of us can be like this—intuitive and open to sensing what others need. Instead of getting caught up in conflicts because we are not on the same page as our kids, trusting our psychic impression to give us the insight and empathy to help smooth over the rough edges is definitely worth trying.

Where there is empathy and everyone is in sync with each other, you have a close-knit family. This feeling can extend out to cousins, friends and people you work with so long as there is a supportive network of souls willing to share their thoughts, feelings and insights with each other. It's an important ingredient that can make your journey through life easier. And, in turn, you can make a difference to their path.

46

ALL IN THE FAMILY

There's a common misconception that psychics are born only into families of psychics. People assume it must be a genetic thing, especially when you hear well-known psychics say, 'Oh, my mother, grandmother, great-grandmother, they all had it,' or that they were 'the seventh child of a seventh child and therefore naturally psychically gifted'.

The truth is that everyone has psychic abilities but in the majority of people they tend to remain untapped. Sure, they shine in particular families where the sixth sense is encouraged or there is a strong karmic predisposition for it. Naturally psychic abilities will be prevalent in these families but this does not mean that other families are not psychic.

What I am trying to say is that your family is also psychic. Your mother and father are psychic, and so are your grandparents, aunts, uncles and cousins! The problem is that they usually didn't recognise their abilities. They often blocked them because they relied on the logical left brain, or they may have grown up in an environment where there has been a social and cultural backlash against all things psychic for centuries. Also, unless you are educated in how to identify and work with your abilities, it can be discouraging to try your hand at something that feels new. The end result is that inherent psychic abilities lie fallow until life opens the doorway. For example, you may have a paranormal experience and then slowly become aware that you do have some ability.

I have been psychic all my life but no one in my family has ever claimed to be psychic. I certainly didn't grow up listening to stories about how psychic my grandmother or others were. If there was any obvious sign of psychic ability, it was kept under cover and never encouraged.

Yet, I know my family is psychic. Mum has great intuition, and I know my father's psychic insights saved his life on at least one occasion. I remember him telling me a story of what happened to him when he was a teenager growing up in a mountain village in Italy during World War II.

He was walking down a narrow cobblestone street late one afternoon when he heard the drone of a swarm of planes approaching the village. Then the explosions began, followed by smoke, fire and screams. Too frightened to run home, he decided to stand where he was, hoping the corner of a building would shield him.

Suddenly, a voice deep inside him said, 'Jump into the barrel.' The voice was so loud that Dad looked around but there was no one there. Then he got a clear picture in his head. It was a psychic vision of himself jumping into an empty wine barrel that was near him. It seemed like a crazy idea but the urge to jump in got stronger until he did just that.

Seconds later the barrel wavered and fell on its side, rolling and gaining speed with every second as it tumbled down the long, steep road with my dad screaming inside. Looking back he laughed at how comical it must have appeared, with his long legs dangling out and the rest of him tucked inside. The barrel kept rolling faster and faster until it finally crashed into the stone wall of a building at the far end of the street. Dishevelled, Dad crawled out and stood on shaky bruised feet. As he swept pieces of broken timber from his clothes he chided himself for being stupid enough to jump in the barrel.

Then the roar of a plane engine pierced his ears, and the screeching sound of a bomb was followed by a split-second of deathly silence . . . before an explosion ripped apart several ancient stone buildings. Numb, Dad looked at the dust and fire and heard the injured crying out in pain. The bomb hit the very spot where he previously stood. Had the barrel not tipped and rolled down the street, my dad would have died.

Yet, when he spoke about events like this, he never put his 'good fortune' down to intuition; it was pure luck or chance. That's because the word 'psychic' really wasn't an everyday concept used by his family or in the village. As in any other area, semantics plays a part in our awareness. If you don't have the right word to describe something, you either can't describe what you experience, or you pin it down to another concept that is less accurate. So, Dad, like most other people in his situation, called those moments when his intuition surfaced 'luck', 'fate', 'chance' or 'coincidence'. It never occurred to him to recognise his psychic ability. And I know many people who still don't recognise their own.

My niece Simone picks up on other people's vibes and has felt the presence of spirits in her room but does not think she is psychic. My sister Lena saw spirits as a child, and my other sister Frances was always spot-on about things like picking fluctuations in the real estate market or getting visions of inventions that only emerged in shops years later. For many years neither thought of herself as psychic; these experiences were 'Oh, you know, just one of those things'. Now, they both openly recognise that they are intuitive, that they do have psychic abilities—and they trust them.

When you look at your own family you might recognise the signs of intuition at work as well.

47
BELIEVE IN THEM

It's refreshing when someone else in the family recognises that they are psychic. They can set a precedent to help your kids feel comfortable with their own abilities. And I know this is the way of the future. The fact that more and more people are opening up to being psychic will give support and encouragement to their family and friends, as Annette's experience confirms.

'I was called the "weird" one by my family, a label that has been with me for most of my life,' she lamented. 'When I was about three, my grandmother was very angry at me when I asked an innocent question. My grandfather had just returned from World War II, and I asked, "Why did the man cut your belly out?"'

All the adults reacted badly—'crazy' was Annette's description. They all became emotional and her grandmother punished Annette by sending her to her bedroom. She didn't understand why everyone had suddenly turned on her. No one explained.

It was only later when she was old enough to understand that they told her. Her grandfather had suffered horrific wounds in a Japanese POW camp. A Japanese soldier had used a sword to gut him, and he spent fourteen months in hospital recovering from the trauma.

'Nobody had told me earlier what happened to Grandad,' Annette said. 'I just knew. I saw it clearly in my head. I don't know what upset them the most—the fact that I was psychic or that I got information that little girls shouldn't know.'

As Annette matured her abilities were obvious but remained unappreciated in her very conservative household.

'I was the "silly" one, the "different" one. People felt uncomfortable with my visions, so it was easier to laugh at me and dismiss what I had to say because it meant they didn't have to confront things or take responsibility,' she said thoughtfully.

'But surely this experience made it easier for your own children and grandkids to accept their psychic abilities,' I asked.

'Yes, it did. I made sure I listened carefully to all their insights. Ricky, my daughter's firstborn, had a knack of knowing what was inside cards. We would give him a sealed envelope and he would tell us what was in it. He would tune in and say things like, "There is fifty dollars in the Christmas card," and then open it and find that he was spot-on. It didn't matter what we put in the card—money, a gift voucher or a gold chain—he intuitively knew what it was.'

Annette challenged adults when she was young and ended up being constantly disciplined and punished for coming out with her truth. She is proud of her intuitive abilities and knows that it takes people like her to help make the path easier for the younger generations and ensure that their insights are not rubbished.

It is the fear of ridicule, and having their precious insights dismissed, that forces lots of psychic kids to block their ability, which is why Annette is careful to nurture them.

'Having been there myself, I feel for them and it reminds me of the humiliation of being labelled "the strange one" because I could hear and see things that others couldn't. I never want to see any of them go into denial, get confused or weaken their psychic ability because others don't understand it,' she said firmly.

Instead, she has encouraged psychic children by supporting them in any way she can. 'If they came out with stories about fairies in the garden, I would say to adults who were ready to laugh at them, "Just because you don't see them, it doesn't mean that they are not there."'

Lily, her great-niece, talks to fairies all the time. And her grandson Alex has frequent spirit visitors and often repeats their messages. Annette recalls that a few years ago he announced that he wouldn't be going to school on Friday and would watch *Finding Nemo* instead. His mother dismissed this and insisted that he would go to school as usual. The following day Alex came home with a note informing parents that there would be a teacher's strike that Friday. Annette laughs as she tells me Alex's intuition was right and that he ended up going to watch the movie. She knows exactly how little Alex feels.

Just because you don't come from a long line of psychics, it doesn't mean that you and your child are not psychic. Obviously, it is easier to work with your abilities if another family member has the same skill set and they are comfortable and open with it. It can then become second nature to you. When there is no precedent, it is not surprising that your psychic ability is often left unrecognised. But it doesn't have to be this way. You can be the one to change the whole dynamic for your family.

48

PERSONAL POWER

Being in control of a situation is always empowering. Gaining personal power is the by-product of knowing what to expect and how to deal with things. Having your child experience a paranormal event can sometimes make you feel unsettled. It can erode your personal power especially when it happens unexpectedly. Suddenly you have to deal with a situation you're not trained to handle. Since you don't know what the rules are, or how to resolve the paranormal incident, you might end up feeling like your hands are tied. What can you do? Who do you turn to?

Help is always on hand for parents of psychic kids. You can seek answers through places like reputable colleges of metaphysics, psychics or even a spiritualist church. Or you can open up and ask your friends and family; they may have the perfect lead.

But there is another avenue you can take, especially when the answers you seek don't necessarily deal with disruptive paranormal experiences. If your child sees a spirit, gets visions of the future, reads your energy or gets a premonition, why not get them to turn inwards for guidance from their soul? You can do the same. If you try it you might be pleasantly surprised to find that your inner self already has the answers.

Turning inward is a journey that most of us have to make in order to reach the depths of the soul. It's worth it. It is an intriguing, fascinating and life-changing journey into the hidden parts of your psyche, into the richness of your soul. Unveiling your spiritual uniqueness is the reward for your efforts.

For psychic kids part of their rite of passage is to explore their inner realm. It doesn't mean that they have to devote themselves 24/7 to such a journey. They can grab snippets of it from time to time as they mature. Your psychic child can unwrap each layer of their inner mystery when they are ready to see, understand and integrate it. Before they reach this stage, they will seek answers in the outer world, referencing people like you and their peers. Being psychic means that they *see*, *feel*, *hear* or *sense* things that are new—sometimes totally foreign or alien to them—but as they start to understand and gain confidence things change. Learning to trust in their psychic impressions, what they are tapping into and how it works can lead them to discover their own personal and even spiritual power.

Spiritual power is an inner connection with the divine that helps them see the beauty and grace in all things. However, when their experiences are challenged or dismissed, they can lose that connection. A child who says, 'I hear voices,' and meets with ridicule can end up questioning their mental health because they know these voices are real, but not to others. Eventually they will learn to shut out the voices, or if they persist they could end up with mental health issues. Now, in some cases the voices could be the signs of conditions like schizophrenia, but it can be the voice of family in spirit or a spirit guide and medical science does not recognise that this is a viable explanation. The child ends up feeling disempowered and it can create confidence issues that linger well into adulthood.

From the age six until nine Jacqui's clairaudient channel was wide open. 'I used to sit alone on the back stairs at home,' she told me. Jacqui found solace there; it was a place where she knew no one would disturb her. Well, no one physical that is.

'I would listen to a "voice" and I talked back to it. I really loved talking to the "voice" because it made me feel good. I believed that I was talking to God,' she told me. It was actually her Spirit guide talking to her. His words comforted her and gave Jacqui a feeling of strength and the hope to carry on as things were difficult at home. The 'voice' became her mentor and friend, a safe haven for the storm in her life.

Your child's sense of personal power is governed by the state of their solar plexus chakra. This chakra also governs free will, manifestation, transmutation and control, self-acceptance and the ego. One of the organs under the domain of the solar plexus is the stomach. Did you know that within the stomach is a knot of brain cells? It's this bundle of nerve endings that triggers your 'gut' feel about things, often making you react to a situation seconds before your physical brain registers it. This is also the centre for personal power.

An underextended solar plexus chakra means that your child's perception of their personal power is diminished; an overextended solar plexus chakra means that they need to feel more control. Either way, these states take away from their power centre. Strengthening the solar plexus chakra, through feeling self-acceptance and confidence, creates a base for them to express their free will and ability to manifest what they want in life. If your child is feeling disempowered you can teach them to restore their sense of personal power with this quick little exercise:

> Ask them to imagine a lovely big yellow bubble over them. Then tell them to bring a bubble of yellow energy into their solar plexus region (or say stomach area) and suggest that this bubble is giving them all the strength and confidence they need. Once they have done that tell them to visualise themselves using this newfound personal power—for example, if they lack confidence at school ask them to visualise themselves standing up in front of the class talking confidently.

When this chakra perception is balanced, your child slowly discovers that not only can they create a little magic in this life but that they are part of the universe. And, just by observing and thinking about it, they will participate in its events and help change them. They will discover that the power of their will is a tremendous force for change. They can change our world. They can infuse it with harmony and balance, acceptance and tolerance. This kind of personal power comes when you know who you are, why you are and that you are connected to everything. Everything is consciousness, everything is interrelated.

This is why it is important that all kids are given the chance to feel comfortable with their abilities, psychic or other. Ultimately, our energies affect everything around us.

49

HOW ABOUT YOU?

You can empower yourself to help your psychic kid. Instead of feeling out of your depth because your kid has an incredible talent, why not become proactive and open up to your own psychic abilities?

Yes, it might be uncomfortable to begin with, because the concept of trusting in your sixth sense is new to you. Look at what thoughts and feelings are holding you back. Is it because of religious, cultural or social beliefs? Perhaps an unsettling experience during childhood makes you reluctant to delve into your psychic abilities? I can appreciate these valid reasons and how it feels easier to simply avoid the topic altogether. However, when they learn to understand what it means to be psychic, many people openly embrace their sixth sense.

What about you? Do you trust your intuition? Are you currently working with your psychic abilities?

The good news is everyone can do it. Here are some helpful tips on what you can do to get the ball rolling.

Becoming self-aware

The first step, a step I feel is important to recommend, is to become self-aware. It doesn't have to take years to do this. All you need to do is set aside some quiet time once or twice a week (yes, I know it is hard for busy parents to find a spare moment, but trust me, it is worth the effort).

Create a relaxing space where you can meditate. You don't need to go into hour-long meditations; ten or fifteen minutes is a good starting point. Put on relaxing music, clear your mind and focus on deep breathing until you feel totally relaxed. When you are in the zone, tune in and look at what fears or doubts block you from accessing your psychic abilities. Don't struggle with this, simply let images from the past surface in your mind and look at what the main theme is.

Once you recognise what's blocking you from tapping into your psychic ability, you have got the perfect platform to clear it so you can move forward.

Acknowledge the thoughts and feelings behind your emotional or psychological block to trusting your intuition. Now, replace it with positive thoughts and visions of yourself actually working with your sixth sense.

This is an easy technique to master and one that will show promising results.

Working with intuition

Intuition, or your inner-tuition, is a natural skill we all have. You often use it without even knowing it. It usually comes as an impression or a feeling of knowing something is right. Since it comes from our mind, we think our head created it, rather than our soul. It's actually a soul impression; your soul feels and knows the answers to things, your brain merely picks it up and relays it to your conscious awareness. So why not put it to the test? Whether you see a vision in your mind's eye, or feel or know something is right, learn to trust it. Learn to trust in your soul. It doesn't matter if you make mistakes as these are learning curves.

Try it out by doing these simple exercises:

• Close your eyes and think about who is the next person who is going to message you on Facebook. Later on, check and see if you were right. If you were right, go back and think about how you felt when you picked up that impression. If you were wrong, remind yourself that it's okay to make mistakes, and try a few more times. Eventually you will get it right. It comes with practice.

• The next time a friend comes to visit, tune into them and see if you pick up how they are feeling and what's been happening to them before they even start talking about their lives. Try this out on a number of friends and see what your strike rate is. Remain positive through the process.

• Visualise what is going to happen to you tomorrow at home or at work. If it comes true, then great. If you are wrong, write down what you visualised—it may actually happen next week, next year or further down the track. Being psychic is amazing but sometimes getting the timing right is tricky.

• Try this exercise with a friend, or even your child if they are more than eight years of age. Visualise a bubble of energy forming in your solar plexus chakra (just below the diaphragm). Concentrate on the bubble and visualise it turning either blue or red. Once it is created, project it out of your solar plexus into your palms and pass it to your friend or child. Ask them to intuitively feel which of the two colours it is. Blue will feel light and breezy, red will feel heavy and warm. Now ask them to create one for you and feel which colour it is.

• Another exercise is to create the energy bubble as above but instead of turning it into a colour, place an emotion in it, for example happy or sad. Get the other person to tune into the emotion you have created in the bubble. Then ask them to create an emotion bubble for you to tune into.

Developing your intuition is easier than you think. It just takes practice, trust and focus. In due time you will start picking up more and more psychic information and eventually you will be comfortable and confident with your own abilities. It will help you keep in step with your child's development.

50

A SALVE FOR LITTLE SOULS

Being a psychic kid has its ups and downs. Having magical moments and getting remarkable insights sometimes comes at a cost. It is occasionally accompanied by feelings of uncertainty that come with breaking through into unknown territory.

When adults confront new situations, they draw on a wealth of past experiences to help them put things into perspective. Psychic kids don't have a huge pool of life experience to draw from to reference things, so putting things into context isn't as easy as ABC. And since these kids see and sense and know so much, it can feel overwhelming when they don't have the right platform to support what they are experiencing. This is where you come in. Applying a salve for their soul is exactly what they need. You can give it to them by providing them with a strong foundation to support their psychic abilities but also to give them a framework to operate in. No matter what happens, they will always feel safe, secure and confident.

One fantastic salve that works wonders is meditation.

Over the years a large number of my own students at the college have taught their kids how to meditate and the results have been tremendous. Some students have created the most amazing soothing and healing meditations, while others have purchased meditation books especially written for kids. Whether you create the meditation yourself, or use an existing meditation, your child will love it.

Meditation is often used to create a sense of relaxing and inner peace. It can help kids offload their worries and feel better after a stressful day. But did you know it can also be used to help kids get in touch with their intuition? I like to think of meditation as downtime for the soul to recharge and also to get insights and visions of what you need to do. This can really help kids clear stress and anxiety, with the added bonus of finding the right answers for life issues.

There are two types of meditation techniques you can teach your child. One is a creative-visualisation meditation, which kids love. A creative-visualisation meditation is where you use your imagination to create the perfect place. It could be by the beach, in flower-studded open fields or even a colourful playground. Whatever your child finds soothing and relaxing can be visually created as a 'downtime' place where they can unwind and feel relaxed and happy. The other technique is a mantra-style meditation. A mantra is a symbol, word, phrase or sound that is repeated over and over again to help quieten the mind.

Here are two very helpful meditations you can try on your kids. I find that guiding them through a meditation works best, so read these meditations out aloud. Before you start, put on some relaxing music, take the phone off the hook and make sure there is nothing to distract your child during the meditation.

Meditation 1: The worry tree

Kids don't always understand why they are stressed, or even how stressed they really are. A stress-release meditation gives them the perfect opportunity to unload stress and create inner calm.

> Take a nice deep breath in and slowly exhale. Take another deep breath in and slowly exhale. Take one more deep breath and slowly exhale.
>
> Now, [your child's name], it's time to relax. You don't have to think about what you need to do later on, for now, just listen to my voice and breathe deeply. As you exhale, feel your body getting more and more relaxed. That's good. [Allow a few minutes for this.]
>
> [Child's name], I want you to see a lovely stream of white light coming down from the sky washing over you. This light will help you feel lighter as you relax. [Allow a few minutes.]
>
> I want you to see yourself walking down a beautiful yellow road that takes you to a lovely field. It is full of bright flowers and big trees. You can hear birds singing and feel the sun on your skin. It's a beautiful place. It makes you feel very happy to be here right now.
>
> I want you to walk over to one of the big trees and you will see a basket by its trunk. [Allow a few minutes.] Now, [child's name], I want you to think about things that have been worrying you—things that have happened at school, or with your friends, and even at home. Anything that has been making you feel upset or sad, I want you to put it into the basket by the tree. This is a worry basket. You can leave all your worries here. [Allow a few minutes.]
>
> The worry tree with its lovely worry basket will take away your worries.
>
> Now that you have let go of these worries, think about all the fun things you would like to do and see yourself doing them. [Allow about five minutes.]

[Child's name], it's now time to come back. You know anytime you feel worried that you can come back to the worry tree and leave your worries in the basket. Take a nice deep breath in and as you breathe out, open your eyes.

Meditation 2: Angelic helper meditation

This is a fantastic meditation to use to help kids call on angelic protection during moments when they are feeling overwhelmed or lost because of what they are experiencing.

Take a nice deep breath in and slowly exhale. Take another deep breath in and slowly exhale. Take one more deep breath and slowly exhale.

[Your child's name], it's okay to relax now and clear your mind. If any thoughts come up, let them float and listen to my voice. Every time you take a deep breath in and breathe out, you are starting to feel relaxed. [Allow a few minutes for this.] That's good.

I want you to visualise a big beautiful fluffy white cloud coming down. See yourself jumping onto this cloud and feeling very comfortable. The cloud is going to lift off now, it's taking you up to a special place where angels live. Just relax and let the cloud take you there now.

[Child's name], the cloud is now in a very beautiful place, can you see it? [Allow a few minutes.] There is an angel coming to meet you. They have a big smile and they are very gentle and caring. If you want, you can ask the angel for their name. [Allow a few minutes.]

This is your protection angel. They are always around you to help you when you feel uncertain about things. You can ask them to help you when you feel lost, lonely or confused. Your angel loves to listen to you. And they love to help you. Why don't you spend a few minutes talking with your angel? You can tell them whatever you want. Whatever you have seen or heard that doesn't make sense, or things that scare you, why don't you let them listen to you? [Allow a few minutes.]

Now, [child's name], why don't you ask the angel to help you change things for the better? Ask them what you can do, or what they can do for you, to give you all the protection and guidance you want. [Allow a few minutes.]

[Child's name], it's now time to come back. You know anytime you want to talk to your angel you can come to this place. They are always here to help you. Take a nice deep breath in and as you breathe out, open your eyes.

Talk with your child after the first few meditations to gauge what they experienced, how it felt to them, if they have any qualms about these meditations, and what advice they got. After a while you won't have to talk about their meditations, just leave the door open for them to share their experiences when they want.

Meditations like this can help your psychic child. Think about other kinds of meditations they can use to help them create a sense of wellbeing. If your child isn't into meditation, there are other supportive actions you can take. Why not talk to other parents and ask them what they do for their kids? Or you can look at things like homeopathy, Bach flowers or bush flower remedies which are fantastic to help shift restrictive thoughts and feelings and help kids deal with underlying issues.

51

CELEBRATING PSYCHIC POWERS

When baby first speaks we celebrate, when they take the first step we applaud and encourage, when they make it through the first day at school we give them a big hug and kiss. These small steps are milestones that are acknowledged and rewarded. But who celebrates when their kid utters their first psychic impression? What do they get? Ignored? Dismissed? When they reveal a premonition, do we cheer them on? If they see the spirit of a loved one, do we happily announce it to others? Why don't we mark these psychic milestones?

Children thrive on positive feedback, praise and encouragement. It gives them the confidence to achieve their dreams. Whether it is standing up and taking that first step or winning a race, their efforts are cherished.

Isn't it time to celebrate their psychic gifts? Give them words of encouragement or other small rewards to show them that you care about their gift. Knowing that their abilities are normal and an asset can have a powerful influence on their wellbeing. It inspires them to trust and explore, to gently unfold their true potential.

Think for a moment: 'How can I be a positive role model to help my child trust in their abilities?'

Let's look at some of the ways you can keep them optimistic and help them navigate through the ups and downs while they learn to master their psychic energies.

Acknowledging

Start by acknowledging their ability. Being psychic is perfectly natural; it's nothing to shun or hide away because others might think it's 'different'. When they see, hear, feel or know something intuitively, encourage them. Obviously, use your intuition to discern whether their imagination is running amok or if they are actually working with their psychic abilities. This means that you will have to trust your own intuition.

Also, reinforce that is okay to be psychic and support that reality. Avoid sending conflicting messages by agreeing with their intuitive impressions one day and then questioning them the next. Be consistent to avoid confusing them.

Building trust

Helping your child trust in their ability is important for their development. It builds their confidence and encourages them to give their psychic abilities another go. As in any other area, when kids receive negative feedback it could act as a deterrent. It may block or even stop them from wanting to work with their gift. Building trust will encourage them to believe in their skill and give them the momentum to keep working at developing their talents.

Setting healthy boundaries

It's important for psychic kids to have healthy boundaries. As you know, kids need routine and structure in their daily lives. Having a routine and structure to support their psychic abilities will help them maintain a sense of balance and harmony. You can teach them some simple steps:

Protecting their energy

If your child is a bit of a psychic sponge, picking up on everyone's thoughts and feelings, teach them to recognise what's theirs and what's not. Get them to visualise a white light washing over them to let go of what's not theirs. Then get them to visualise a golden bubble that maintains their personal boundary.

Nourish

The pineal gland, a tiny acorn-shaped gland in the head, is responsible for our psychic impressions as it activates the third-eye chakra. It is largely hollow and contains water and small crystals. Over time poor nutrition can cause calcification of the pineal gland which means that your psychic abilities will begin fading away. A diet high in white sugar, white flour, heavily processed foods and excessive fluoride will affect the health of the pineal gland. You can help your psychic kid keep this wonderful gland working at its optimum by nourishing their body with healthy and nutritious foods.

Time for practice/time for sleep

Set aside special time for them to practise working with their intuition so it doesn't disrupt their sleep routine. Teach them to tell their spirit guides not to let too much spirit activity happen while they're asleep at night.

Cutting of cords

If they feel 'yucky' energies hooking into their aura, get them to visualise white scissors cutting away these energy cords and gently sending them back to wherever they came from.

Coping with changes

Being psychic is natural but it can bring change into children's lives. Why not talk about some of the things that might change within them as they develop their skills? You might discuss things like:

Dealing with others' reactions

Some people feel uncomfortable listening to psychic messages in general so if your child reveals an insight that does not go down well, don't take it personally. If they raise a few eyebrows running around talking about seeing dead people, don't be fazed. Realise that these people do not understand what it means to be a psychic kid. Explain to your child that people see things differently but if they do not share their view, honour their differences. If their own friends judge them, give your kids a few coping skills like positive affirmations to say to themselves to help maintain their sense of self and confidence.

Opening new pathways

Your child might start opening new pathways; instead of just hearing Spirit they might start physically seeing spirit visitors or getting clairvoyant images. Keep a line of communication open so they can tell you when something new has happened, allowing you to offer your suggestions or help as required.

Go with the flow

It's helpful to run with your psychic experiences but it's also beneficial to know when to stop, regulate or change a situation. Teach your child to allocate a time and place to focus on their psychic impression so it does not interfere when they are doing an important task that requires their full attention. For example, if they are trying to cross the road, or they are in the middle of an exam, being distracted by what's going to happen in the future might not be appropriate. Obviously, if their sixth sense is helping them avoid an accident when they cross the road, or help them get the right answer in an exam, of course let it flow! If they tell their spirit guides to work with them after school or before school, then they can have a lovely routine.

Encourage

Kids thrive on encouragement. Whether it is in the classroom or on the sporting field, positive encouragement from parents, teachers and peers gives them the feel-good factor. Making them feel good about working with their abilities helps keep them open to talking about and sharing their experiences with you so you can gauge where they are at.

Reward

When a teacher gives them a gold star, or they get a ribbon or trophy for sporting events, the result is a sense of satisfaction for a job well done. Think of ways you can reward them when they achieve something special psychically. It also reinforces the message that being psychic is part of who they are.

Your encouragement can make the difference between your child growing into an open, enthusiastic and confident psychic or becoming confused and uncertain about what they sense and feel. A smile, hug and a few positive words will sustain them through the ups and down of developing their psychic skills. Your child will lap up the attention and positive feedback. If I heard 'That's fantastic, darling, you're doing a great job,' instead of 'I don't want to hear about it,' my childhood psychic experiences would have been so much better.

Engage in your kid's psychic activity when you can—it really drives home the message, 'I believe in you'.

52
KIDS ON THE GO

When I hold a newborn baby I don't just see a body. I see a soul packaged in a tiny body. I see a soul who has left the spirit world and begun an incredible journey on earth. The newborn baby is tactile — they connect to me through their six senses. They do not understand what is going on around them. They *feel* it. They feel my energy. Just being in each other's energy creates a soul connection that does not need words. Parents of newborns understand this. Babies can't use words to convey what they want. Sure, they can cry but they have a range of different cries. Which cry is saying what? You learn pretty quickly how to let your instinct kick in to tell you what kind of cry it is, what they are trying to say and need. Your instinct is usually spot-on, right? And your child intuitively responds to your energy, to the vibe given off by your thoughts and feelings.

What I love about newborns is that their energy is pure and full of unconditional love. Their pure soul is protected by a divine golden bubble. This bubble is called the birth mantle. It acts as a protective buffer zone to shield their soul from absorbing disruptive energies that may be in their environment, such as restrictive thoughts and feelings in people's auras or residual energy in a room. The birth mantle also protects their immature chakras while they develop during the first three months of life.

While a baby is wrapped up in the beautiful golden cocoon, it is also in the care of a network of spirits who oversee their wellbeing. Newborns still spend a lot of time in the spirit world. They astral-project back 'home' while they are still learning to integrate into the physical world. Also, during this phase, your child's chakras need time to develop and open up. Once these centres of consciousness are open and working properly, the birth mantle bubble disintegrates and their soul is now fully integrated into the physical realm. Even though the birth mantle has dissolved, it is reassuring to know that angels and spirit guides are waiting in the wings and keeping a careful eye on your baby.

Perhaps you have sensed their presence lingering by the cot? If you have, that's great. But if you haven't, why not try to feel them? Open up and talk to them about your child. Let them enlighten you about what special gifts your child has and what path they will follow in life.

If you want, you can go a little further and ask them to show you the unity consciousness energy. These are rays of consciousness that stream into the world daily. These rays are important because they awaken our awareness by triggering our chakras, and from time to time you might feel that internal shift happening. You know, when you get that a-ha moment of self-awareness or a piece of the puzzle falls into place. Certain cultures like the Mayans knew about these rays.

The Mayans, who are known for their predictive Mayan calendar, believed that rays of consciousness influenced our collective destiny. They defined periods in time, or ages, by the resonance given off by these rays. It is believed that in 1999 the world was flooded with the eighth ray, which resonates at a frequency that is helping to dissolve the collective filters, to break down our thinking barriers, and help us shift more into the feminine right side of the brain. This is evolution unfolding right before our very own eyes! Isn't it interesting that the psychic indigo children emerged under this ray?

The Mayans believe that we moved into the ninth ray during 2011 and this significant shift will bring forth the highest frequency resonance, known as the unity consciousness, into our reality. It is dissolving more of the perceptual filters and this will help us learn to work with both left and right hemispheres of the brain equally, which means more and more of us will become aware of our psychic potential. This universal energy will help us let go of feeling duality, the division between the rulers and the ruled, which kept us in a state of separation; it didn't foster unity between us.

This evolutionary energy will help us unify the world if we want. However, since we are on the cusp of this energy, and it will run for years to come, we will see an increase in chaos, confusion and conflict as the old power structures, which no longer serve humanity, will crumble. Astrologers would say this is the work of the transformative energies of the planet Pluto. Pluto is the great purger that awakens the unconscious and ploughs the fields of your mind to help your soul release outdated beliefs and patterns. Its energy is to destroy what no longer serves you, so you can transform by giving birth to a new part of you. In 2012 Neptune, the planet that rules spirituality and psychic abilities, returns to its sign of

Pisces and this will send positive vibes to help people awaken and develop their psychic abilities for years to come.

The children of today are kids on the go—they have a lot to achieve. They are the ones who will bring unity consciousness into our world and I welcome that energy and the dedication of these young souls who have incarnated at this time to help our world grow.

53

LITTLE TEACHERS

Life is an ever-changing kaleidoscope of events designed to help you to push personal boundaries in order to grow. Some of these experiences show you how to develop patience, tolerance and acceptance. Others teach you how to stretch your beliefs and embrace new ideas. One of the most engaging life lessons happens when the tables are turned and you suddenly find that you are the student and your child becomes the teacher.

Children can teach you a thing or two about our changing world. Each generation does, although we often don't see children in that light. But if you look back at your own childhood, you will see how you did things differently to your parents. Kids in your generation were an evolutionary force that reshaped the foundations set by your parents, and their parents before them. Successive generations are like the pounding ocean that forever changes the foreshore of outdated perceptions. In its wake, a fresh landscape emerges, one that's primed for new beginnings.

The current wave of children are incredibly advanced and savvy and highly psychic as the result of this natural progression. Growing up in such a technological environment means these kids are connected with the world in ways we couldn't imagine during our own childhoods. In particular, their psychic connection to their higher self and spirit guides is finely tuned and this makes them fantastic teachers. Many of them are trying to teach us how to catch up with their inbuilt wisdom and knowledge, like Susana's son David when he was four years old.

'I know he came here to teach me about spirituality,' Susana told me. 'David was the one, the messenger sent to basically save me. I am not being dramatic. This is what I feel. And that's exactly what his name means, "a gift from God". When David was four he was a horrendous eater. I had to put him in the bath and feed him while he was playing with toys and the bubbles. One day, out of the blue, he said, "Mummy, there is a little baby girl coming."'

At that time Susana had recently remarried and wanted to enjoy time with her new husband. She wasn't planning for a baby.

David said, 'I have chosen her for you, Mummy.'

'I had no idea what he was talking about, so I asked him, "How do you know all this?" His big, soft brown eyes looked up at me. "Because I saw her. In heaven there is a room where lots of babies are and I went there and chose her for you. She's coming down soon."'

Susana said, 'Okay,' and left it at that.

Five months later she fell pregnant unexpectedly. Her daughter, Krysta, was an unsettled baby who cried constantly.

'I hope I chose the right baby, Mummy,' David said after one particularly trying day. 'This one cries a lot.'

David continued to be fussy eater. 'We got into a ritual, almost. When he got in the bath he would go into some sort of trance. I'd be trying to feed him and I would have to stop because he was talking like an old soul. He was only four and he would say the most incredible stuff like, "Mummy, I came here to help you go home."'

On one occasion, he told Susana, 'You came to Earth a long time ago. Your spaceship crashed and you lost your memory. You don't know who you are. You have been here for so long that your eyes are covered in mud and you can't see where you are going. When I was in heaven there were five of us.'

'David, what do you mean there were five of us?' Susana asked him.

'I was one of the brothers and I was watching you doing this and so I decided to come here and help you to make sure you go to heaven this time,' he said.

'Why, honey?'

'Because it's taking so long and you seem to be getting more lost.'

Susana was stunned by what she heard. She knew about past lives and reincarnation but she'd never discussed it with David.

When she asked him why he hadn't told her this before, he replied simply, 'Because you never asked. Now that you are asking me, I'm telling you.'

'Why me? Why did you choose to help me out of all people? Was it because Mummy would believe you?'

David got out of the bath, got dressed and asked his mother for some pencils and paper. He proceeded to draw a picture of a planet.

'This is where we come from,' he said, his young voice tinged with an air of authority. 'I came from here,' he said, pointing to the planet. 'And now I am here,' he said as he drew a second planet representing Earth. 'I'm here to help people that are lost find to find their way home.'

Some mothers would think that David's imagination was running wild, but not Susana. She listened intently to every word.

She asked him if he remembered his name while he lived on that planet.

'Dajet,' he replied. 'I'm here to help the planet, Mummy.'

Susana realised David was a star child. A star child is a soul who has memories of a previous incarnation on a different planet. There are lots of star children being born today. Their arrival coincides with a shift in how people feel about their place in the bigger scheme of things; more people are beginning to believe that we're not alone, that life exists in other parts of the universe. Quantum physics is making amazing discoveries about other dimensional realities and helping us to join the dots. But it is the star children who will introduce us to technologies that will connect us to the universe.

What also amazed Susana was David's intuitive knowledge about energy. He has 'healing hands' and even knew how to energetically cleanse a house without being shown. In fact, Susana herself didn't know much about auras and energy back then; she's only recently started learning about them.

When David was six he said, 'Mummy, you put your beautiful energy in yucky things.'

'Darling, what are you talking about?' she asked.

'You mix it. Once you mix it, it's really hard to bring it back,' he explained. 'I never mix my energy.'

'What do you do?'

'I keep it clean. It's very easy to be peaceful but it's hard to stay peaceful when other people are fighting,' he said.

'How do you stop it from happening?' she asked.

'When everyone is fighting and there is a yucky energy, I always say to myself, "I have my beautiful energy and I don't want to mix it." Then I start singing my special song and in my mind I go to a beautiful place where I am doing my favourite things. I don't listen to them fighting. I don't mix my energies because it is hard to clean dirty energy.'

Susana realised that psychic children are advanced beyond their years because they have the ability to tap into their cellular memory and listen to their spirit guides. They can also see and feel energy and even instinctively know how to use it to suit their needs. There is so much you can learn from your little teacher. Are you ready to be a student?

Psychic kids are simply amazing! They see, hear, feel and know about things that lie beyond our everyday perception and that is something to be treasured. Their skills include clairvoyance, clairaudience, clairsentience, telepathy, healing and mediumship. Regardless of which sixth sense skills they draw upon, your child is extraordinary.

Let's celebrate psychic kids. They are not unusual or weird but precious souls who are part of an ever-growing wave of souls incarnating on Earth with fantastic intuitive abilities that will help redefine our perceptual reality. These incredibly wonderful and gifted children have come to join us in an exciting period of accelerated change because they hold the seeds for a new beginning. Like all psychic kids, your child has a mission. They are here to teach us how to open up to our own psychic abilities and to see the world through new eyes. One thing is for sure—our psychic children will leave a long and lasting impression on the pages of history. We are so lucky to have our psychic kids join us on this wonderful journey of life.

APPENDIX

Colour ready reckoner

The colours in your aura reveal your physical, emotional, mental and spiritual wellbeing. A healthy aura glows with clear, luminous colours and white light, all vibrating at their true harmonic resonance. Each colour present in the aura reflects a different emotional and psychological characteristic. For example, someone with a predominantly yellow aura generally tends to experience and reflect upon life through their intellect.

Even though each colour of the spectrum represents a general characteristic, tonal variation in a colour highlights specific thoughts and feelings that we're experiencing at the moment. Consider the colour red. It's such a physical colour, isn't it? But it represents more than physical vitality and action.

RED
If you've got deep dark reds in the aura, this indicates that you could be experiencing some sort of nervous upheaval or that your temper is getting the better of you or you're feeling physically restricted. A clear red suggests that you're actually moving through your anger, while gentle reds indicate that you're feeling at ease with the physical aspects of your life and are in balance. Rose red hues suggest strong passion and feelings of love, while rose pinks indicate that you're currently working with compassion towards others. When there's lots of pink in the aura, it means you're working with unconditional love.

ORANGE
The presence of oranges in the aura reflects the

state of your emotional landscape. Bright clear oranges suggest that you are feeling emotionally balanced and comfortable with intimacy. Rust or murky oranges can suggest blocks that can be the source of illness so pay attention to what part of the body the murky orange energy is over. For example, if it is over the knee then knee problems may well eventuate in the near future. Rust or murky oranges indicate that deep-seated fears and traumas need to be released in order to restore health and wellbeing. Consider repressed emotions or fear about moving forward with life. Salmon colours can indicate a healthy intimate relationship, while peach means you are feeling okay with your ambitions.

YELLOW

A strong vibrant yellow means you are optimistic or you are sitting in your power. It can also mean that you have been doing a lot of thinking, or you rely on your mental body more than your emotional body to make decisions. Soft pastel yellows suggest joy and happiness. Yellow with a touch of lime hues indicates that you are working with your head and heart. Russet yellows

indicate that you are feeling weak-willed or disempowered; they can also suggest repressed anger. Golden yellows mean that you are feeling loved and empowered to help others. An absence of yellow indicates lack of wisdom and tolerance. Yellow with black spots can represent unfounded fear.

GREEN

A lovely clear green means that you are feeling self-nurtured and loved. There is a sense of growth in your life. You are giving and receiving love equally. Lime green indicates that you express your power in a loving way. Jade green suggests that you are speaking your truth in a loving way. You are caring and compassionate. You could be sending healing to another. Dark murky greens indicate a lack of self-love or nurturing to self or others, or a lack of empathy.

BLUE

A strong clear blue indicates feelings of tranquillity and a sense of freedom. It also suggests that you are communicating well. You are being expressive and creative. You are comfortable with speaking your personal truth.

Blues tending towards the indigo hues indicate that you are drawing your insights from a higher source. Dark murky blues suggest that you are feeling uncomfortable in saying what you need to say, or that you are speaking your truth but no one is listening. You might be feeling judged by others, or you are displaying a lack of discernment.

INDIGO

A lovely ray of indigo in your aura means you are working with your intuition. You are seeing things clearly and you are getting insights and visions that can help you make choices that are right for you. Indigo with a touch of violet to it means that you are using your insights to help others or to see the bigger picture. Dark murky shades of indigo mean you are blocking your perception; you might be deluding yourself about something or you are listening to others' insights and overriding your own impressions.

VIOLET

Violet in your aura suggests that you are feeling very connected to life and to the bigger picture. It means you are exercising wisdom and grace. You could be going through a period of self-transformation. You are tapping into a higher consciousness or awareness. Violet shades with a touch of red suggest you are able to ground the information you are getting from a higher source. Murky shades of violet indicate that you are feeling disconnected from others and the source, that the two parts of you—the lower and higher selves—are in a state of separateness. Violet with touches of pink indicates a love of humanity. Purple shades like lavender represent a deeper connection with Spirit.

WHITE

The presence of white reflects an inner self of truth and purity. If it presents as bubbles or a head shape in the upper part of the aura, it can indicate the presence of your spirit guide.

GOLD

Gold energy within the aura indicates a strong level of protection and also a lovely connection to Spirit or someone who is in the service of humanity.

SILVER

Silver can indicate that you are integrating new wisdom and knowledge.

BLACK

Black in the aura can mean you have restrictive thought-forms, or blocks, so please look at your health. It can represent feelings of the absence of light in your life. Sometimes it can suggest that you want to forget things or that your ambitions have been thwarted.

NOTES

[1] Shanti Devi story from the article written by Dr K.S. Rawat in *Venture Inward* magazine, March/April, 1997.

[2] Daniel Tammett quoted in Richard Johnson, 'A genius explains', *The Guardian*, 12 February 2005, <www.guardian.co.uk/theguardian/2005/feb/12/weekend7.weekend2>

[3] ibid.

[4] ibid.

NOTES

Shanti Devi story from the article written by Dr K.S. Rawat in
Venture Inward magazine, Mar/Apr 1997.

Daniel Tammet quoted in Richard Johnson, A genius explains,
The Guardian, 12 February 2005, <www.guardian.co.uk
the guardian/2005/feb/12/weekend7.weekend2>

ibid

ibid